Steven N. Gold, PhD
Jon D. Elhai, PhD

Trauma and Serious Mental Illness

Trauma and Serious Mental Illness has been co-published simultaneously as *Journal of Psychological Trauma,* Volume 6, Numbers 2/3 2007.

Pre-publication REVIEWS, COMMENTARIES, EVALUATIONS . . .

"**A** TRULY GROUND-BREAKING VOLUME that is likely to engender controversy, as it challenges a culturally well-accepted myth that trauma is irrelevant to the lives of people living with psychosis. The authors have carefully, empirically, documented that while biology plays an essential role in the development of a psychosis, the presence of trauma exposure, particularly childhood trauma exposure, is also a crucial aspect of the trajectory toward psychosis for many. Finally, the hidden trauma in the lives of seriously and persistently mentally ill adults is exposed in such a way that no clinician can deny its existence, or the importance of addressing it clinically. . . . Takes our understanding of psychosis beyond the simply biological and places it in the realm of the biopsychosocial."

Laura S. Brown, PhD, ABPP
Director
Fremont Community Therapy Project
Seattle, WA

Trauma and Serious Mental Illness

Trauma and Serious Mental Illness has been co-published simultaneously as *Journal of Psychological Trauma,* Volume 6, Numbers 2/3 2007.

The Journal of Psychological Trauma is the successor title to the *Journal of Trauma Practice*, which changed after Vol. 5, No. 4, 2006. The *Journal of Psychological Trauma*, under its new title, begins with Vol. 6, No, 1, 2007.

Trauma and Serious Mental Illness, edited by Steven N. Gold, PhD, and Jon D. Elhai, PhD (Vol. 6, No. 2/3, 2007). *"A truly ground-breaking volume that is likely to engender controversy, as it challenges a culturally well-accepted myth that trauma is irrelevant to the lives of people living with psychosis. The authors have carefully, empirically, documented that while biology plays an essential role in the development of a psychosis, the presence of trauma exposure, particulary childhood trauma exposure, is also a crucial aspect of the trajectory toward psychosis for many. Finally, the hidden trauma in the lives of seriously and persistently mentally ill adults is exposed in such a way that no clinician can deny its existence, or the importance of addressing it clinically. . . . Takes our understanding of psychosis beyond the simply biological and places it in the realm of the biopsychosocial." (Laura S. Brown, PhD, ABPP, Director, Fremont Community Project, Seattle, WA)*

Trauma and Dissociation in a Cross-Cultural Perspective: Not Just a North American Phenomenon, edited by George F. Rhoades, Jr., PhD, and Vedat Sar, MD (Vol. 4, No. 1/2 and 3/4, 2005). *Examines the psychological, sociological, political, and cultural aspects of trauma and its consequences on people around the world.*

Prostitution, Trafficking, and Traumatic Stress, edited by Melissa Farley, PhD (Vol. 2, No. 3/4 2003). Prostitution, Trafficking, and Traumatic Stress *documents the violence that runs like a constant thread throughout all types of prostitution, including escort, brothel, trafficking, strip club, and street prostitution. The book presents clinical examples, analysis, and original research, counteracting common myths about the harmlessness of prostitution. It explores the connections between prostitution, incest, sexual harassment, rape, and battering; looks at peer support programs for women escaping prostitution; examines clinical symptoms common among prostitutes; and much more.*

Trauma Practice in the Wake of September 11, 2001, edited by Steven N. Gold, PhD, and Jan Faust, PhD (Vol. 1, No. 3/4, 2002). *"Extraordinarily timely and important. . . . It is now a different world that confronts mental health professionals. This book presents both broad theoretical perspectives and the personal accounts of some who have required care and those who provide it. It begins to help us understand the changes of the post 9/11 era–how domestic terrorism has affected the national psyche as well as individuals, inflicting new wounds and awakening old hurts." (James A. Chu, MD, Director, Trauma and Dissociative Disorders Program, McLean Hospital, Belmont, Massachusetts; Editor,* Journal of Trauma & Dissociation*)*

Trauma and Serious Mental Illness

Steven N. Gold, PhD
Jon D. Elhai, PhD
Editors

Trauma and Serious Mental Illness has been co-published simultaneously as *Journal of Psychological Trauma,* Volume 6, Numbers 2/3 2007.

HMTP

The Haworth Maltreatment & Trauma Press®
An Imprint of The Haworth Press

www.HaworthPress.com

Published by
The Haworth Maltreatment & Trauma Press, 10 Alice Street, Binghamton, NY 13904-1580
USA.
The Haworth Maltreatment & Trauma Press is an imprint of The Haworth Press, 10 Alice Street,
Binghamton, NY 13904-1580 USA.

Trauma and Serious Mental Illness has been co-published simultaneously as *Journal of Psychological Trauma,* Volume 6, Numbers 2/3 2007.

The development, preparation, and publication of this work has been undertaken with great care. How-ever, the publisher, employees, editors, and agents of The Haworth Press and all imprints of The Haworth Press, Inc., including The Haworth Medical Press® and The Pharmaceutical Products Press®, are not responsible for any errors contained herein or for consequences that may ensue from use of ma-terials or information contained in this work. With regard to case studies, identities and circumstances of individuals discussed herein have been changed to protect confidentiality. Any resemblance to actual persons, living or dead, is entirely coincidental.

The Haworth Press is committed to the dissemination of ideas and information according to the highest standards of intellectual freedom and the free exchange of ideas. Statements made and opinions ex-pressed in this publication do not necessarily reflect the views of the Publisher, Directors, management, or staff of The Haworth Press, Inc., or an endorsement by them.

Library of Congress Cataloging-in-Publication Data

Trauma and Serious Mental Illness / Steven N. Gold, Jon D. Elhai, PhD, editors
      p. cm.
      Co-published simultaneously as Journal of psychological trauma, v. 6, no. 2-3, 2007.
      Includes bibliographical references and index.
      ISBN-13: 978-0-7890-3650-6 (hard cover : alk. paper)
      ISBN-13: 978-0-7890-3651-3 (soft cover : alk. paper)
      1. Psychoses–Etiology. 2. Psychoses–Treatment. 3. Psychic trauma–Complications. 4. Post-traumatic stress disorder–Complications. I. Gold, Steven N. II. Elhai, Jon D. III. Journal of psy-chological trauma.
        [DNLM: 1. Psychotic Disorders–etiology. 2. Psychotherapeutic Processes. 3. Psychotic Dis-orders–therapy. 4. Stress Disorders, Post-Traumatic–complications. 5. Stress Disorders, Post-Trau-matic–therapy. WM 200 T7772 2007]
      RC512.T737 2007
      616.85'21–dc22   2007032779

The HAWORTH PRESS Inc.
Abstracting, Indexing & Outward Linking
PRINT *and* ELECTRONIC BOOKS & JOURNALS

This section provides you with a list of major indexing & abstracting services and other tools for bibliographic access. That is to say, each service began covering this periodical during the year noted in the right column. Most Websites which are listed below have indicated that they will either post, disseminate, compile, archive, cite or alert their own Website users with research-based content from this work. (This list is as current as the copyright date of this publication.)

(continued)

(continued)

Bibliographic Access

- *Cabell's Directory of Publishing Opportunities in Psychology <http://www.cabells.com>*

- *MediaFinder <http://www.mediafinder.com/>*

Special Bibliographic Notes related to special journal issues (separates) and indexing/abstracting:

- indexing/abstracting services in this list will also cover material in any "separate" that is co-published simultaneously with Haworth's special thematic journal issue or DocuSerial. Indexing/abstracting usually covers material at the article/chapter level.
- monographic co-editions are intended for either non-subscribers or libraries which intend to purchase a second copy for their circulating collections.
- monographic co-editions are reported to all jobbers/wholesalers/approval plans. The source journal is listed as the "series" to assist the prevention of duplicate purchasing in the same manner utilized for books-in-series.
- to facilitate user/access services all indexing/abstracting services are encouraged to utilize the co-indexing entry note indicated at the bottom of the first page of each article/chapter/contribution.
- this is intended to assist a library user of any reference tool (whether print, electronic, online, or CD-ROM) to locate the monographic version if the library has purchased this version but not a subscription to the source journal.
- individual articles/chapters in any Haworth publication are also available through the Haworth Document Delivery Service (HDDS).

As part of
Haworth's
continuing
commitment
to better serve
our library
patrons,
we are
proud to
be working
with the
following
electronic
services:

AGGREGATOR SERVICES

EBSCOhost

Ingenta

J-Gate

Minerva

OCLC FirstSearch

Oxmill

SwetsWise

FirstSearch

Oxmill Publishing

SwetsWise

LINK RESOLVER SERVICES

1Cate (Openly Informatics)

ChemPort
(American Chemical Society)

CrossRef

Gold Rush (Coalliance)

LinkOut (PubMed)

LINKplus (Atypon)

LinkSolver (Ovid)

LinkSource with A-to-Z (EBSCO)

Resource Linker (Ulrich)

SerialsSolutions (ProQuest)

SFX (Ex Libris)

Sirsi Resolver (SirsiDynix)

Tour (TDnet)

Vlink (Extensity, formerly Geac)

WebBridge (Innovative Interfaces)

ChemPort

LinkOut.

ULRICH'S
RESOURCE LINKER

SerialsSolutions

TOUR

((extensity))

WebBridge

Trauma and Serious Mental Illness

CONTENTS

CLINICAL APPLICATIONS

ABOUT THE EDITORS

Steven N. Gold, PhD, earned his doctoral degree at Michigan State University in 1981, and his bachelor's degree at Washington University in St. Louis. He is Professor at Nova Southeastern University (NSU) Center for Psychosocial Studies, and founded and serves as Director of the Trauma Resolution and Integration Program (TRIP) at NSU's Community Mental Health Center. TRIP provides psychological services to adults experiencing difficulties related to a history of child abuse, single event trauma occuring in adulthood, or dissociative symptoms. TRIP also offers doctoral-level training and conducts ongoing research on trauma-related topics. Dr. Gold is the President-Elect for the trauma division (56) of the American Psychological Association.

Dr. Gold's book *Not Trauma Alone: Therapy for Child Abuse Survivors in Family and Social Context* delineates the treatment model employed at TRIP. Dr. Gold has published and presented extensively on abuse, trauma, and dissociation. He is co-editor of *Trauma Practice in the Wake of September 11, 2001* and served as guest editor of a special issue of the APA journal *Psychotherapy* about psychological trauma. He is editorial consultant and ad hoc reviewer for a number of professional journals.

Dr. Gold is a past president of the International Society for the Study of Dissociation (ISSD). He is a Fellow of ISSD and of the American Psychological Association, and a member of the International Society for Traumatic Stress Studies and the Society for the Advancement of Sexual Health. He holds certification in clinical hypnosis with the American Society of Clinical Hypnosis and is a Certified Traumatologist through Florida State University's Traumatology Institute.

Jon D. Elhai, PhD, is Assistant Professor in the Disaster Mental Health Institute and Department of Psychology at The University of South Dakota. He earned his PhD from Nova Southeastern University, and completed his internship and postdoctoral fellowship at the Medical

University of South Carolina and Charleston Veterans Affairs Medical Center. Dr, Elhai has published numerous scientific articles and book chapters on traumatic stress, and has presented his work at several national and international conferences. He has served as Managing Editor of the *Journal of Trauma & Dissociation*, an editorial board member for the *Journal of Traumatic Stress*, and an ad hoc reviewer for several additional journals. He was the 2003 recipient of the International Society for Traumatic Stress Studies' Chaim Danieli Young Professional Award. He is a member of the American Psychological Association and the International Society for Traumatic Stress Studies.

Trauma and Serious Mental Illness

Trauma and Serious Mental Illness has been co-published simultaneously as *Journal of Psychological Trauma,* Volume 6, Numbers 2/3 2007.

Trauma and Serious Mental Illness:
Is the Pendulum About to Swing?

Steven N. Gold

For enough decades now, that many of our junior colleagues may not be aware that it was ever otherwise, we have known that serious mental illnesses (SMIs)–most notably schizophrenia and bipolar disorder–are a manifestation of disordered biochemistry. Before we knew this to be the case, in an earlier, now all-but-forgotten era, a prevalent belief was that these and other syndromes were not reflections of neurotransmitter malfunction, but responses to horrific experiences. In the glow of current scientific knowledge, the long-outdated notion that the major contributor to SMIs was nurture rather than nature may appear at best quaint and at worst terribly misguided.

A logical extension of the conclusion that SMIs are biologically-based disorders is that treatment must consequently be biologically based as well. Therefore, the primary intervention approach for these disorders has been pharmacological. Those in treatment for SMIs are routinely told that their disorder is chronic, and that unless they continue taking their medication for the rest of their lives, their symptoms will unquestionably worsen. And because it is widely assumed that people with SMI diagnoses are experiencing the effects of disordered biochemistry, for the most part mental health professionals have stopped

Steven N. Gold, PhD, is Professor, Nova Southeastern University (NSU) Center for Psychological Studies, and Director, Trauma Resolution and Integration Program (TRIP), NSU Community Mental Health Center.

[Haworth co-indexing entry note]: "Trauma and Serious Mental Illness: Is the Pendulum About to Swing?" Gold, Steven N. Co-published simultaneously in *Journal of Psychological Trauma* (The Haworth Maltreatment & Trauma Press, an imprint of The Haworth Press) Vol. 6, No. 2/3, 2007, pp. 1-5; and: *Trauma and Serious Mental Illness* (ed: Steven N. Gold, and Jon D. Elhai) The Haworth Maltreatment & Trauma Press, an imprint of The Haworth Press, 2007, pp. 1-5. Single or multiple copies of this article are available for a fee from The Haworth Document Delivery Service [1-800-HAWORTH, 9:00 a.m. - 5:00 p.m. (EST). E-mail address: docdelivery@haworthpress.com].

listening to what these people have to say, dismissing their reports as manifestations of disturbed thinking.

But–is the evidence that serious mental illnesses are biologically-based as incontrovertible as we have been led to believe? By taking seriously what people diagnosed with SMIs have to say, the authors of many of the pieces assembled here directly or indirectly call that seemingly firmly established conclusion into question. What these works suggest, on the basis of empirical evidence and clinical observations, is that the extreme disturbances in psychological adjustment comprising SMI may, in whole or in part, be reactions to the extreme and extremely disturbing circumstances embodied by psychological trauma.

One of the values of the trauma field in general is that it reminds us that many of the otherwise perplexing anomalies in behavior encountered by mental health professionals may become comprehensible when viewed as responses to certain types of experiences or learning histories. The writings found here apply that general principle to the realm of SMI. Through various lenses–theory, research and practice–they investigate and provide evidence for various linkages between SMIs and psychological trauma.

Paul Hammersley, John Read, Stephanie Woodall, and Jacqueline Dillon address the broad issue of the relationship between psychosis and childhood trauma. Reviewing the research in the context of the history of thinking about psychopathology, they describe a recent and growing body of literature showing a strong relationship between childhood trauma and psychotic disorders. In addition, they present a case illustrating how psychotherapy can lead to appreciable reduction in distress and symptomatology, and improvement in functioning in individuals with SMI.

Colin A. Ross examines the overlap between, and possible confounding of, psychotic disorders with dissociation. He delineates how the premise that psychotic disorders are biologically based biases the conceptual framework, questions, and methodology that shape empirical investigation of SMIs, as well as their diagnosis and treatment. He identifies flaws in the conceptual framework and gaps in the empirical evidence, related to the prevailing belief that psychosis is primarily biologically based, and shows how much of the earliest literature on schizophrenia, dating back to Bleuler, describe symptoms that would more accurately be classified as dissociative than schizophrenic. In closing, he makes a number of recommendations, including suggestions for future research that would provide initial steps in working toward better delineating the distinction between psychotic and dissociative syndromes.

Andrew Moskowitz and Dirk Corstens, like Ross, address the relationship between psychosis and dissociation, and the relationship of the latter to trauma. However, their specific focus is on auditory hallucinations. They meticulously trace the history of thinking about auditory hallucinations to question the widely-held belief that these experiences fall into two categories that distinguish psychosis from dissociation. Their conclusion, that hearing voices is diagnostic of dissociation rather than of psychosis, is for the most part consistent with Ross's perspective on the relationship between these two classes of disorders.

The piece by Jan Faust and Lindsay M. Stewart examines, from both a theoretical and an empirical perspective, the relationship of psychosis to the quality of family of origin environment and to age of onset of childhood abuse. Psychoanalytic theory has long held that the more pervasive and earlier disruptions in development are, the more likely they are to result in psychotic forms of adjustment. Faust and Stewart found a number of differences consistent with this conception between two groups of children in treatment for the adverse affects of abuse: one diagnosed with PTSD, and one that met criteria for a psychotic disorder. The psychotic group reported appreciably earlier onset of abuse and described their families as more conflict-ridden than did the PTSD group. In addition, mothers of the psychotic children endorsed a lower degree of cohesiveness in the family than did mothers of the children with PTSD.

A study by Anouk L. Grubaugh, Karen J. Cusack, Eunsil Yim, Rebecca G. Knapp and B. Christopher Frueh differs in a crucial respect from the other works presented here. Most of the other authors examined the prospect that severe trauma is a precursor to SMIs. Grubaugh and colleagues investigated how SMIs, and in particular being placed in residential treatment for SMIs, can be a risk factor for traumatization. In general, their findings were consistent with the revictimization literature: In-patients of both genders who had experienced prior interpersonal violence were more likely than those without such a history to report victimization while in residential treatment. Although there was not a relationship found between victimization in residential treatment and PTSD, they note that high levels of trauma in the sample generally may have rendered actually existing differences difficult to detect. One of the important practical implications of this study is the vulnerability of in-patients to traumatization both within and outside of residential treatment, and the need to implement measures to prevent such maltreatment.

Benjamin F. Levy, a psychiatrist at a university health center, offers a detailed examination of clinical situations in which individuals meet criteria for both bipolar and trauma-related disorders. He presents a comprehensive, thoroughly referenced consideration of the overlap between bipolar and trauma-related disorders. His central point is that in instances where criteria for both types of syndromes are met, psychotherapy for the trauma-related disorder in conjunction with pharmacological intervention for bipolar symptoms can lead to sufficiently extensive and stable resolution that medication can eventually be discontinued. Levy describes five case histories to illustrate how this dual approach to treatment can be implemented and the outcomes that can result.

Last but certainly not least, Bertram P. Karon explicates a psychoanalytically-oriented conceptual and treatment model grounded in the premise that schizophrenia can be best understood as "chronic terror disorder." Among the authors found here, Karon is unquestionably the patriarch of the perspective that SMIs are reactions to severe trauma. Since the 1970s, he has often been a lone voice countering the conviction that SMIs are exclusively biologically-based disorders, and advocating for their treatment with psychotherapy, which he has long argued is "the treatment of choice" for schizophrenia (Karon & VadenBos, 1981). It is fitting, therefore, that he should have "the last word" on the topic of SMIs and trauma. Here, he provides a sweeping overview of the thesis that he has been promulgating and developing for over 30 years. Weaving together theoretical, clinical, and empirical literature with case examples, he makes a compelling case that schizophrenia is a treatable response to "devastating traumas," and that psychotherapy can be tremendously effective for people diagnosed schizophrenic if it is rooted in a willingness to "listen, hear, and help."

Perhaps the wide-spread acceptance as established fact that SMIs are exclusively biologically-based was premature, and not grounded in empirical evidence as solid as we have been led to believe. Perhaps lived experience makes a greater contribution to SMIs than has been commonly acknowledged for several decades now. Perhaps, if empirical and clinical investigation supports these premises, the pieces assembled here are harbingers of a "swing of the pendulum" back to a more balanced and accurate perspective on the origins and effective treatment of SMIs.

REFERENCE

Karon, B.P. & VandenBos, G.R. (1981). Psychotherapy of schizophrenia: The treatment of choice. New York: Aronson.

CONCEPTUAL FRAMEWORKS

Childhood Trauma and Psychosis:
The Genie Is Out of the Bottle

Paul Hammersley
John Read
Stephanie Woodall
Jacqueline Dillon

SUMMARY. After one hundred years of denial and ignorance, it was finally accepted 20 years ago that sexual, physical, and emotional abuse of

Paul Hammersley, BA (hons.), MSc, BABCP (accred.), RMN, is Programme Director for Post-Graduate Studies, COPE Initiative, School of Nursing Midwifery and Social Work, University of Manchester, United Kingdom (E-mail: paul.hammersley@manchester. ac.uk).

John Read, PhD, is Senior Lecturer, Psychology Department, University of Auckland, Private Bag 92019, Auckland, New Zealand (E-mail: j.read@auckland.ac.nz).

Stephanie Woodall, BSc, MSc, RMN, is Cognitive Behavioural Therapist (psychosis), Department of Psychology, North Staffordshire Combined Health Care, United Kingdom (E-mail: Stephanie.woodall@ntlworld.com).

Jacqueline Dillon, is National Chair, United Kingdom Hearing Voices Network (E-mail: Jaquidillon333@aol.com).

[Haworth co-indexing entry note]: "Childhood Trauma and Psychosis: The Genie Is Out of the Bottle." Hammersley et al. Co-published simultaneously in *Journal of Psychological Trauma* (The Haworth Maltreatment & Trauma Press, an imprint of The Haworth Press) Vol. 6, No. 2/3, 2007, pp. 7-20; and: *Trauma and Serious Mental Illness* (ed: Steven N. Gold, and Jon D. Elhai) The Haworth Maltreatment & Trauma Press, an imprint of The Haworth Press, 2007, pp. 7-20. Single or multiple copies of this article are available for a fee from The Haworth Document Delivery Service [1-800-HAWORTH, 9:00 a.m. - 5:00 p.m. (EST). E-mail address: docdelivery@haworthpress.com].

7

children, along with neglect, was a genuine and common phenomenon with potentially devastating long term consequences for the mental health of the survivors. Until recently, there has been one exception to this rule. Sufferers of psychotic experiences were excluded. Their distress was caused predominantly by genetics or biology, or so they were told. Recent research has shown this to be a fallacy. Some of the recent studies even suggest that psychosis is the diagnostic category most likely to have experienced severe childhood trauma. This paper summarizes the historical context and offers a précis of the most important recent research findings. In keeping with the ethos of this journal we offer a case study to illustrate the effectiveness of psychotherapy for trauma survivors with psychosis. We end with an appeal to collaborate with the users movement to take this agenda forward. doi:10.1300/J513v06n02_02 *[Article copies available for a fee from The Haworth Document Delivery Service: 1-800-HAWORTH. E-mail address: <docdelivery@haworthpress.com> Website: <http://www.HaworthPress.com> © 2007 by The Haworth Press, Inc. All rights reserved.]*

KEYWORDS. Childhood trauma, schizophrenia, psychosis, therapy

After a century of denial, neglect, and inflexible dogmatic thinking from the psychiatric establishment, the crucial relationship between trauma in childhood and subsequent adult psychosis is finally being recognized. Freud's reversal of his initial observation that every single one of his patients suffering from "hysteria" had a history of premature sexual experience, led to a later theory of fantasy and childhood projection. Until comparatively recently, this set of circumstances, coupled with Western politico/medical ideology and the voracious appetite of the pharmaceutical industry, fostered the perception of sufferers of major psychotic illness not as individuals with a life narrative, but as a form of sub-species defined by misfiring synapses and aberrant genetics.

This situation has now changed permanently. Consider the following five events occurring during the last calendar year; three occurring in the United Kingdom, one in the United States, and one in Scandinavia.

1. At a recent debate at The Maudsley Institute of Psychiatry in London, two of the authors (JR and PH) proposed the motion, "This House believes that child abuse is a cause of schizophrenia," to an audience composed primarily of researchers and clinicians, with a smattering of. "patients" and family members. After summaries of the relevant re-

search and the usual genetically oriented counter arguments, followed
by a full discussion, the motion was carried by 114 votes to 52.

2. In the July edition of the influential *British Medical Journal,* Professor
David Kingdon from Southampton University produced an article detailing the failure of first and second-generation anti-psychotic medications and calling for an about-turn in the treatment of psychosis, "there
is now evidence to support psychological targets for interventions, for
instance experiences of childhood physical and mental trauma"
(Kingdon, 2006, p. 212).

3. Earlier in 2006, The Royal College of Psychiatrists in the UK commissioned an article on the subject of "When where and how" to ask individuals with serious mental illness about adverse life experiences
(Read, Hammersley, & Rudegeair, 2007).

4. In November 2005, *Acta Psychiatrica Scandinavica* published the first
full literature review of more than 40 studies detailing the significant relationship between childhood trauma and psychosis. The review was
described by prominent British psychologist Oliver James as "an earthquake that will rapidly change the psychiatric profession" (James, 2006)

5. Most surprising of all were the comments made in August 2005 by the then
president of the American Psychiatric Association, Steven Sharfstein.

> There is widespread concern at the over-medicalization of mental
> disorders and the over use of medications. Financial incentives and
> managed care have contributed to the notion of a "quick fix" by taking a pill and reducing the emphasis on psychotherapy and
> psychosocial treatments. There is much evidence that there is less
> psychotherapy provided by psychiatrists than 10 years ago. This is
> true despite the strong evidence base that many psychotherapies are
> effective used alone or in combination with medications. . . . If we
> are seen as mere pill pushers and employees of the pharmaceutical
> industry, our credibility as a profession is compromised. . . . As we
> address these Big Pharma issues, we must examine the fact that as a
> profession, we have allowed the bio-psycho-social model to become
> the bio-bio-bio model. (Sharfstein 2005, p. 3)

The battle has not been won, but the tide has certainly turned. The
story of how this remarkable (and still ongoing) reversal of opinion has
taken place begins with the feminist movement of the late 1970s and
early 1980s. Before anyone could research the relationship between
childhood abuse and psychosis, it was first necessary to establish that

child abuse was real, common, and had potentially devastating consequences for the psychological well being of the victims.

THE POLITICAL HISTORY

In her memorable book *Rocking the Cradle of Sexual Politics: What
Happened When Women Said Incest,* Louise Armstrong (1994) gives an
insider's view of the mainstream psychiatric, political, religious, and le-
gal establishment responses to the explosion of revelations of childhood
abuse in the early 1980s. The initial response was complete denial, The
American Medical Association in 1975 estimated prevalence of incest
in the USA to be one per million (Read, Van Os, Morrison, A., & Ross,
2005). Armstrong (1996) reports how attempts to publish accounts of
childhood trauma would be rejected by publishers on the grounds that
the problem was so incredibly rare that there would be no market for
such a book.

The second response was the claim that abuse did exist, but its consequences were minimal, a position adopted by the prominent researcher
of sexual behaviour Alfred Kinsey as far back as 1953. When it became
clear that in fact there were serious long term physical and psychological problems associated with childhood trauma, the next stage was
blaming the victims. Child victims of sexual abuse, even young children, were portrayed in the press, psychiatric/psychological journals
and courts of law as prematurely sexual, provocative, 0 and partly
guilty. This particular attempt at obfuscation had a relatively short life.
Blaming the mothers of the children involved, however, was a more
successful tactic for the "abuse deniers." Mothers of sexual abuse victims found themselves portrayed as sexually inadequate and as actively
consenting to the sexualization of their own children. This led to the almost unbelievable situation where many mothers of abused children
found themselves in the courts of law accused of neglect in their duty of
care, and losing custody battles (Armstrong, 1996).

Evidence about the huge scale of the issue continued to grow. In a final throw of the dice, blame was shifted to one professional group: therapists. Therapists of all theoretical backgrounds were blamed for
planting false memories of abuse into their clients and destroying the
lives of families. False memory associations, all over the world, were
given brief but very sympathetic press coverage. These Associations
are now so small in membership that they are widely viewed as scientifically and politically irrelevant. (E.g., The New Zeland branch, Casual-

ties of Sexual Allegations, folded in 2002 after just a few years of unsuccessfully trying to convince the public that there was an "epidemy" of false allegations.)

At the end of this lengthy process a form of consensus was reached. Child abuse was clearly related to severity of psychiatric illness in terms of earlier first admissions, longer and more frequent hospitalizations, longer time in seclusion, more medication, higher symptom severity, more frequent self-harm, and more frequent suicide (Read, Goodman, Morrison, Ross, & Aderhold, 2004). This understanding was applied to individuals with diagnoses of depression, anxiety, substance misuse, sexual dysfunction, eating disorders, personality disorders, and PTSD.

There was one glaring exception. Psychiatry in general and biological psychiatry in particular, refused to accept the significance of trauma in the lives of individuals diagnosed with psychosis. Before and during "the decade of the brain," adverse childhood and adult life experiences were deemed irrelevant or reduced to the roles of mere triggers of an underlying biological or genetic vulnerability (Read, Mosher, & Bentall, 2004).

THE EARLY RESEARCH

Pioneering research in the 1990s that began to loosen the cork entrapping the genie of the relationship between childhood trauma and psychosis was often hampered by a lack of resources, and sometimes suffered from methodological problems such as small sample size, inconsistency in definition, and trauma data often based on patients' retrospective self-report, which was considered (incorrectly) by some to be a questionable source of reliable information. This research has been covered in detail elsewhere (Larkin & Morrison, 2006; Read et al., 2004; Read et al., 2005). This article will instead concentrate on some of the recent major studies that have ensured the genie's escape from the bottle.

1. Bebbington and Colleagues (2004)

This was a huge general population study conducted in the UK. A sample of 8,580 British adults was assessed for psychiatric disorders using structured assessments by neutral researchers, separate from the research team, drawn from the Office of Population Census and Surveys. The interviewees were asked to state whether they had ever experienced any of nine "victimization experiences" clearly defined and displayed on cards. The nine victimization experiences were: sexual abuse, bullying, running away from home, time in local authority care, time in a childhood institution, expulsion from school, homelessness, violence at work, serious injury, or assault.

Significant associations were found between all but one of the victimization experiences (expulsion from school) and subsequent psychosis. The strongest association was between sexual abuse and psychosis. Those in the psychosis group were 15 times more likely to have experienced sexual abuse than those without psychiatric problems. In addition, contrary to popular opinion, childhood trauma was three times more strongly associated with psychosis than with adult neurosis or with drug or alcohol misuse. The authors concluded that this excess of "victimization experiences" in the lives of psychotic patients was suggestive of a social contribution to the cause of psychosis.

2. Janssen and Colleagues (2004)

This study conducted in Holland is arguably the most significant study to date in the psychosis/trauma research agenda. Like in the previous study, the sample size was large. The research team attempted to eradicate the issue of self-report of childhood abuse from psychotic individuals by initially interviewing a sample of 4,045 individuals who were "psychosis free" at initial interview about their childhood experiences. The participants were then re-assessed after three years to see who had made the transition into psychosis. In this study, psychosis was rated by four clinicians according to three levels of severity: 1. Any psychosis, 2. Pathology level psychosis, and 3. Needs level psychosis (intervention required). The results were unequivocal. Participants who had been abused were 3, 13, and 11.5 times (respectively) more likely than the non-abused to develop psychosis during the study period.

This study was able to demonstrate much more. The researchers controlled for possible confounding variables in their analysis. After controlling for age, sex, educational level, employment status, urbanicity, ethnicity, marital status, presence of previous psychiatric diagnosis, psychosis in a first degree relative and drug use, the significant relationship was maintained. Those in the abused sub-group were 2.5, 9, and 7 times more likely to have developed the various levels of psychosis. Note that controlling for a family history of psychosis and still finding a significant relationship demonstrates that adverse events can increase one's chances of becoming psychotic without a genetic predisposition.

One final aspect of the Janssen study warrants attention. The researchers were able to assess severity of abuse in addition to occurrence of abuse. The results demand attention. People who had experienced child abuse of mild severity were twice as likely as non-abused participants to have "pathology level" psychosis, compared to 10 and 48 times for those who had suffered moderate and high severity of abuse respectively. This is the clearest evidence to date of both the "dose-response effect" and of actual causality.

3. Spataro, Mullen, Burgess, Wells, and Moss (2004)

This is the most controversial of the three studies, and our interpretation of the data is certainly at odds with that of the authors. In this study, 1,612 individuals, who had formally documented histories of severe abuse, were identified from the records of the Victoria Institute of Forensic Medicine in Victoria Australia. The participants were then followed up as adults for analysis of treatment in the public mental health system. The traumatized group was then compared with a general population group. The great strength of this study is that it completely negates concerns about the accuracy of self-report and is able to control for some confounding variables. Unlike the two previous studies, the relationship between childhood trauma and schizophrenia was non-significant. In addition, no relationship was found between childhood trauma and subsequent adult substance or alcohol misuse. Both findings are highly unusual in that they contradict a large body of previous research, suggesting problems with both the methodology of the study and the sample.

There were indeed a number of major methodological problems associated with the study. First, the certain presence of a proportion of individuals in the general population group who would have experienced abuse in their childhoods introduces a systematic bias into the results. Second and more important is the issue of age. The average age of the subjects was early twenties. This is simply too young to determine whether or not an individual will become psychotic. For example, in twin studies of schizophrenia, the cut-off age for establishing concordance is usually 40 years (twice the age of this study) and statistics are adjusted accordingly. In addition, the general population sample was significantly older than the abused sample and as such had a greater chance of developing psychosis. These and other failings were identified by the authors themselves.

Finally and most importantly, a key point was missed by the original researchers. The fact that all the individuals in the traumatized group had been identified by the authorities at the time of their abuse means that all the children had told someone and, moreover, had been believed (appropriately), and that a large proportion would have been removed from the abusive situation. In addition, some would have received support and even therapy. Such scenarios are rare and predict good outcome. We would argue that, far from demonstrating that child abuse is not associated with adult psychosis, the Spataro study actually may be construed as providing evidence that removing children from abusive situations may actually be highly protective of onset of psychosis in adulthood (Read & Hammersley, 2006).

4. Whitfield, Dube, Felitti, and Anda (2005)

This retrospective survey of 17,337 Californians found, for both men and women, that childhood physical abuse, childhood sexual abuse, childhood emotional abuse, neglect, and several other adverse childhood events, including witnessing your mother being battered, significantly increased the risk of experiencing adult hallucinations. After controlling for substance abuse, gender, race, and education, those who had experienced the greatest number of types of adverse events in childhood were 4.7 times more likely to have experienced hallucinations. We concur with the researchers' conclusions that:

> Our data and those of others suggest that a history of child maltreatment should be obtained by health care providers with patients who have a current or past history of hallucinations. This is important because the effects of childhood and adulthood trauma are treatable and preventable. . . . Finding such a trauma-symptom or trauma-illness association may be an important factor in making a diagnosis, treatment plan, and referral and may help patients by lessening their fear, guilt or shame about their possibly having a mental illness. (Whitfield et al., 2005, p. 810)

PSYCHOTIC MOOD DISORDER

The schizophrenia spectrum disorders are not the only major mental health problems in which psychotic symptoms such as hallucinations and delusions are a feature. Major mood disorders such as bipolar disorder and unipolar psychotic depression may also have psychotic features. The life experiences of individuals with psychotic mood disorders have not been the subject of systematic investigation. This is a serious omission. If a correlation between childhood trauma and psychosis could be established in the major mood disorders, this would suggest a genuine, consistent cross-diagnostic effect.

Hammersley, Dias, Todd, Bowen Jones, Reiley, and Bentall (2002) found that in a group of bipolar disordered patients with doubly ratified diagnosis, drawn from a national research trial, there was a highly significant association between childhood trauma and psychotic symptoms. This association was strongest in relation to sexual trauma and adult auditory hallucinations. This finding has been replicated by Fox and Reid (in preparation). In addition we have found an almost identical pattern in unipolar psychotic depression (Hammersley & Fox, 2006).

Moving Forward

We will never be able to improve the care offered to service users experiencing the symptoms of psychosis until we have the courage to ask them about their life experiences. Service users want and expect us to do so (Lothian & Read, 2002). A training programme developed in New Zealand (Cavanagh, Read, & New, 2004) that equips mental health workers to ask about and respond appropriately to disclosures of trauma is to commence in the UK and possibly Canada, in the near future.

Recovery is possible, and lives can be reclaimed. To illustrate this we offer the case study of a cognitive behavioural "trauma informed" intervention delivered by one of the authors (SW) to an individual diagnosed with schizophrenia that resulted in full symptom remission and discharge from mental health services. The user's name and identifying information have been altered to protect her anonymity.

Veronica

Psychiatric History. Veronica has been involved with psychiatric services with a diagnosis of schizophrenia since the death of her father, when she was 28 years old. She has had three psychiatric admissions to hospital in the last three years following thoughts of self-harm. Veronica has been told that the cause of the problem is a brain abnormality.

Personal History. Veronica's personal history was characterized by familial violence, bulled severely at school, parental separation, death of father by suicide, raped as an adult.

Description of Presenting Problems. Veronica described hearing a male voice, which she interpreted as telling her to kill herself, by saying "come and get it done," "hurt yourself," and "you are useless." She viewed the experience as being of a highly critical and bullying nature, possibly perpetrated by a ghostly spirit (a friend of her ex-partner). Veronica described "hearing voices" mainly when in a highly aroused state, often in public areas, or when alone in her flat. Thoughts focused upon impending danger, and fears of going mad or committing self-harm. These thoughts maintained high levels of anxiety. She reacted by scanning the environment to check for danger, which heightened anxiety further and led to thoughts of loss of control. Eventually she would leave the situation.

Goals. To not harm herself or carry out the voice's instructions.

1. To manage/cope better with her voice experience.
2. To attempt to understand her experience and seek a diagnosis.
3. To not self harm or responding to the voices

   Precipitants to Psychotic Phenomena.

1. Social situations/crowds whereby her hypervigilant cognitions were activated, resulting in high levels of arousal, and making her believe she was in danger.
2. Being alone in her flat, whereby her cognitions related to personal safety were activated.
3. Any mood changes influencing her arousal and voice activation.
4. Images/memories being activated (e.g. father's death) which resulted in high arousal and changes in cognitions and voice activation.
5. Beliefs of danger, failure, worthlessness, could activate the voice.

Onset. Veronica described having begun to hear voices following a violent assault (rape) approximately three years ago by her boyfriend at the time. She did not press charges and the relationship ended. She continued to have fears of his return to harm her, the worst imagined outcome being murder.

Cognition. Thoughts were concerned with her fears of "going mad" and carrying out the act of self-harm. However, she reported being able to resist instructions and has some control.

Affect. Veronica described feelings of low mood and depression and high levels of anxiety, including palpitations, breathlessness, and restlessness. These experiences occurred most often when she feels vulnerable (e.g., being alone in her flat at night, large social gatherings or crowded places).

Maintenance. The cycle was maintained by safety behaviours, including anger, swearing, shouting at the voices, thought suppression, avoidance of situations, and high levels of arousal. In addition, beliefs such as "I am in danger, a failure, not good enough," "I'm different," "the world is unsafe," served to maintain the anxiety. Eventually she would leave the situation and avoid the perceived impending disaster. She was unable to disconfirm her beliefs of "danger and fears" of going mad and harming herself.

Intervention. The main emphasis of the intervention was to enable Veronica to talk about her story and develop a warm and trusting relationship, before any direct therapeutic work could occur. Then, the initial aspect of the work focused upon coping strategy enhancement in the attempt to reduce her arousal levels as Veronica was struggling to cope on a daily basis and had limited social functioning. This entailed utilizing Veronica's own resources to reduce her arousal levels; interestingly, this enabled her to gain some control over her symptoms and maximised some early success.

Sharing the formulation and introducing the PTSD model had an empowering effect as Veronica began to make sense of her experiences and made connections between past events and present distress. She was also able to cluster her problems, which helped to reduce the hopeless feelings she had about her problems being insurmountable. As she became more confident to manage some of her distress, Veronica gradually began to drop some of her safety behaviours which seemed to maintain her distress. An educational approach was selected to work on her hypervigilance in social settings and the impact upon her arousal levels and cognitions. This prepared her for the behavioural experiments to follow.

A hierarchy of situations was identified whereby Veronica could gradually introduce herself to test out her predictions of "going mad" without using safety behaviours and from not avoiding the situation. If she did have voice activation, she utilised self-statements to de-arouse herself before entering the feared situation and occasionally throughout. She eventually had repeated successes but retained some doubt about the possibility that under certain situations she may still go mad. A lot of emphasis was placed on normalizing and humanising her experiences. She began to realize that she could cope during difficult circumstances. This raised her self-esteem and enhanced her social functioning.

Veronica has continued using these skills and managing her anxiety and depression effectively. As a result of this de-arousal, she is in control of her voices. Social networks have improved and she has begun to acknowledge her own resilience. She has had no further hospital admissions.

CONCLUSION

We have made good progress but there is still much to do. Much of the credit for this progress must be attributed to the users movements from all over the world who continue to provide support and inspiration to the fast growing number of professionals, who are determined, now that the genie is out of the bottle, to never let it be forced back in. The last word, therefore, goes to Jacqui Dillon, the National Chair of the UK "Hearing Voices" network, who issued this press release on the day of the debate at The Institute of Psychiatry (Dillon, 2006).

> In our experience, gained through more than 15 years running a national network, listening to people who hear voices, many of them living with a diagnosis of schizophrenia; it is clear that there is a definite link between traumatic life events and psychosis.
>
> On a daily basis, we hear terrible stories of sexual, emotional and physical abuse, and the impact of racism, poverty and stigma on people's lives.
>
> We do not seek to reduce people to a set of symptoms that we wish to suppress and control with medication. We show respect for the reality of the trauma they have endured, and bear witness to the suffering they have experienced.
>
> We honour people's resilience and capacity to survive often against the odds.
>
> The reduction of people's distressing life experiences into a diagnosis of schizophrenia means that they are condemned to lives dulled by drugs and blighted by stigma, and offered no opportunity to make sense of their experiences. Their routes to recovery are hindered.
>
> Rather than pathologizing individuals, we have a collective responsibility to people who have experienced abuse, to acknowledge the reality and impact of those experiences and support them to get the help they need.
>
> Abuse thrives in secrecy. We must expose the truth and not perpetuate injustice further. Otherwise today's child abuse victims will become tomorrow's psychiatric patients[s10].

REFERENCES

Armstrong, L. (1994). *Rocking the cradle of sexual politics: What happened when women said incest.* Reading, MA: Addison-Wesley Publishing Company.

Bebbington, P., Bhugra, D., Brugha, T., Singleton, N., Farrell, M., Jenkins, R., et al. (2004). Psychosis, victimization and childhood disadvantage: Evidence from the second British national survey on psychiatric morbidity. *British Journal of Psychiatry, 185,* 220-226.

Cavanagh, M., Read, J., & New, B. (2004). Childhood abuse inquiry and response: A New Zealand Training programme. *New Zealand Journal of Psychology, 33,* 137-144.

Dillon, J. (2006, April 6). Child abuse, trauma and mental illness. *Dare to Dream.* Retrieved April 17, 2007, from http://www.dare-to-dream.us.

Fox, R. M., & Reid G., S. (In preparation). A study of the relationship between childhood trauma and symptom profiles in bipolar disorder.

Hammersley, P., Dias, A., Todd, G., Bowen Jones, K., Reiley, B, & Bentall, R.. (2002). Childhood trauma and hallucinations in bipolar affective disorder: A preliminary investigation. British Journal of *Psychiatry, 182,* 543-547.

Hammersley, P., & Fox, R. (2006). Childhood Trauma and Psychosis in the Major Mood Disorders. In W. Larkins & A. Morrison (Eds.). *Trauma and psychosis: New directions for theory and therapy.* New York: Routledge.

James, O. (2006, June). *Child abuse can cause schizophrenia.* Neurointerests. Retreived April 17, 2007 from http://www.neurointerests.com/.

Janssen, I., Krabbendam, L., Bak, M., Hanssen, M., Vollebergh, W., de Graaf, R., et al., (2003). Childhood abuse as a risk factor for psychotic experiences. *Acta Psychiatrica Scandinavica, 109,* 38-45.

Kingdon, D. (2006) Psychological and social interventions for schizophrenia. *British Medical Journal, 333,* 212-213.

Larkin, W., & Morrison, A. (2006). *Trauma and Psychosis.* London: Routledge, 2006

Lothian, J., & Read, J. (2002). Asking about abuse during mental health assessments: Clients" views and experiences. c*New Zealand Journal of Psychology, 33,* 137-144.

Read, J., Goodman, L., Morrison, A., Ross, C., & Aderhold, V. (2004). Childhood trauma, loss and stress. In J. Read, L. Mosher, & R. Bentall (Eds.), *Models of madness: Psychological, social and biological approaches to schizophrenia.* London: Routledge.

Read, J., & Hammersley, P. (2006). Can very bad childhoods drive us crazy: Science, ideology, and taboo. In J. Johannessen, B. Martindale, & J. Cullberg (Eds.). *Evolving psychosis.* London: Routledge.

Read, J., Hammersley, P., & Rudegeair, T. (2007). Why, when and how to ask about childhood abuse. *Advances in Psychiatric Treatment, 13,* 101-110.

Read, J., Mosher, L., & Bentall, R. (2004). *Models of madness: Psychological, social and biological Approaches to schizophrenia.* London: Routledge.

Read, J., Van Os, J., Morrison, A., & Ross, C. (2005). Childhood trauma, psychosis and schizophrenia: A literature review with theoretical and clinical implications. *Acta Psychiatrica Scandinavica, 112,* 330-350.

Sharfstein, S. (2005). Big pharma and american psychiatry: The good, the bad and the ugly, *Psychiatric News, 40,* 3-4.
Spataro, J., Mullen, P., Burgess, P., Wells., & Moss, S. A. (2004). Impact of child sexual abuse on mental health: Prospective study in males and females. *British Journal of Psychiatry, 184,* 416-421.
Whitfield C. L., Dube, S. R., Felitti, V. J., & Anda, R. F. (2005). Adverse childhood experiences and hallucinations. *Child Abuse and Neglect, 29,* 797-810.

doi:10.1300/J513v06n02_02

Dissociation and Psychosis:
Conceptual Issues

Colin A. Ross

SUMMARY. The relationship between dissociation and psychosis is not a topic of serious study and research in the psychosis field, though it has received attention in the dissociation literature. A number of conceptual problems must be solved before the role of dissociation in schizophrenia and other psychoses can be a central issue in diagnosis, research and treatment. These include problems with: the model of mind-body interaction accepted in psychiatry, definitions of dissociation and psychosis, the concept of pseudo-hallucinations, DSM criteria for schizophrenia, research measures for dissociation and psychosis, the sociology of psychiatry, the drug industry, assumptions about etiology of dissociation and psychosis, and assumptions about treatment. These problems are discussed and recommendations are made for DSM-V and future research. doi:10.1300/J513v06n02_03 *[Article copies available for a fee from The Haworth Document Delivery Service: 1-800-HAWORTH. E-mail address: <docdelivery@haworthpress.com> Website: <http://www.HaworthPress.com> © 2007 by The Haworth Press, Inc. All rights reserved.]*

Colin A. Ross, MD, is affiliated with The Colin A. Ross Institute for Psychological Trauma, 1701 Gateway, Suite 349, Richardson, TX 75080 (E-mail: rossinst@rossinst.com).

[Haworth co-indexing entry note]: "Dissociation and Psychosis: Conceptual Issues." Ross, Colin A. Co-published simultaneously in *Journal of Psychological Trauma* (The Haworth Maltreatment & Trauma Press, an imprint of The Haworth Press) Vol. 6, No. 2/3, 2007, pp. 21-34; and: *Trauma and Serious Mental Illness* (ed: Steven N. Gold, and Jon D. Elhai) The Haworth Maltreatment & Trauma Press, an imprint of The Haworth Press, 2007, pp. 21-34. Single or multiple copies of this article are available for a fee from The Haworth Document Delivery Service [1-800-HAWORTH, 9:00 a.m. - 5:00 p.m. (EST). E-mail address: docdelivery@haworthpress.com].

KEYWORDS. Psychosis, schizophrenia, dissociation, trauma

The relationship between dissociation and psychosis is multi-faceted and complex (Ross, 2004). It is important conceptually, and for research, psychometrics, diagnosis, and treatment. The relationship between dissociation and psychosis is not clear in the DSM-IV-TR (American Psychiatric Association, 2000), and should be addressed in the DSM-V. I will discuss a number of conceptual issues concerning the relationship between dissociation and psychosis, and will then make a number of recommendations for future thought and research. I have provided full references for these points elsewhere (Ross, 2004).

CONCEPTUAL ISSUES

The Model of Mind-Body Interaction in Contemporary Psychiatry: The Concept of "Underlying Pathophysiology"

Biological psychiatry is currently dominated by a reductionist model of mind-body interaction that pays lip service to the biopsychosocial model. Symptom expression can be triggered or colored by culture and experience, within biological psychiatry, but causality for serious mental disorders is allowed to run in only one direction: from brain to mind. Aberrations in the brain are allowed to cause aberrations in the mind, but not vice versa.

Etiology of serious mental disorders, then, begins in the biology of the organism, with abnormal DNA. The expression of the abnormal DNA results in abnormal cellular biology, which causes abnormal thoughts, feelings and behavior. Mind is an epiphenomenon of brain; and the future of psychiatry lies in understanding the biology of mental disorders, and intervening at the biological level. Psychosocial interventions can be at most adjunctive.

When this model dominates, dissociation is relegated to the status of epiphenomenon, "hysterical reactions" or neurosis. The relationship between dissociation and psychosis cannot be an important problem because dissociation belongs to a trivial category. Psychosis, on the other hand, is regarded as severe, biological, scientific, medical, and worthy of significant clinical and research attention.

The concept of "underlying pathophysiology" lies at the core of contemporary biological psychiatry. For instance, Carter (2006) states that, "the neural systems underlying impaired cognition in schizophrenia need to be" (p. 356).

Similarly, Onitsuka and colleagues (2006) suggest that, "the fusiform gyrus is the site of a defective anatomical substrate for face processing in schizophrenia[s1]" (p. 455). In most of biological psychiatry, the concept of "underlying pathophysiology" is unquestioned. It is impossible to speculate, within this paradigm, that "underlying psychological trauma" could be the cause of abnormal brain structure and function.

Although it still dominates the field, the bioreductionist version of biological psychiatry is beginning to be questioned, for instance by Keith (2006), by Turkington, by Kingdon and Weiden (2006), and by Read, Mosher and Bentall (2004). Even bioreductionists are beginning to allow the reversal of brain defects by environmental input, although only in the form of medication. For instance, McDonald and colleagues (2006) speculate that there could be "genetically mediated hippocampal deficits . . . associated with bipolar disorder but reversed in patient groups because of the neurotrophic effects of treatment with mood stabilizers[s2]" (p. 484).

Immediately preceding this statement, McDonald and colleagues (2006) stated that possible causes of hippocampal volume reduction in bipolar mood disorder include, besides abnormal DNA, "obstetric complications and stress-induced glucocorticoid excess." Here one sees a brief, partial recognition of the possibility that a person with normal DNA could develop brain abnormalities in response to traumatic experience, and then undergo reversal of these abnormalities due to therapeutic input from the environment.

In principle, such environmental input could include psychotherapy. That possibility can be allowed only in a fully biopsychosocial and bidirectional model of brain-mind interaction. In a truly biopsychosocial model, none of the three dimensions is more fundamental or "underlying" than the other two. It is possible for a genetically normal individual to experience brain damage from psychological trauma that is reversible with psychotherapy.

If such a model was accepted, then all studies of hippocampal volume reduction in all diagnostic categories, including bipolar mood disorder and schizophrenia, would have to consider the possibility that the hippocampal damage is due to a genetically normal response to trauma, and not to endogenous "underlying pathophysiology." The contribution of genes and environment to hippocampal volume reduction could vary across disorders and individuals from fully genetic to fully environmental. The relative roles of genome and environment in a given individual would have to be determined empirically, and could not be known scientifically on an *a priori* basis. Until such a bidirectional causal model of the brain-mind field is widely accepted in psychiatry, dissociation will be relegated to the periphery, and its relationship to psychosis will not be regarded as a serious problem.

Definitions of Dissociation and Psychosis

The definitions of dissociation and psychosis, one might say, are dissociated. For instance, in the psychosis section of DSM-IV-TR the word *dissociation* does not appear once, and dissociative disorders are not considered in the differential diagnoses of psychoses. This is due to both the implicit and the explicit definitions of the two terms. Implicitly, dissociation is defined as a psychological defense mechanism, while psychosis is a symptom of brain disease. Although DSM-IV-TR is supposed to be atheoretical, implicitly endorsed theories of etiology dominate the organization of the manual: dissociative disorders are not considered in the differential diagnoses of psychotic disorders, in part, because dissociation and psychosis are regarded as belonging to separate categories.

For this situation to be corrected, both dissociation and psychosis must be shorn of their ideological and etiological histories. Both must be truly phenomenological in their definitions. Confusion arises because there are several different meanings of dissociation (Ross, 2000; 2004). Dissociation at times means reported symptoms and observed behaviors. At other times, it means a postulated defense mechanism. On other occasions, a general systems meaning of dissociation as a disconnection between variables is endorsed. Finally, dissociation can be a technical term in cognitive psychology. The defense mechanism of dissociation is only one possible cause of the phenomenon of dissociation, that is, of dissociative symptoms. There is no reason, in principle, why a given dissociative symptom, in a given individual, could not be caused by abnormal DNA or brain chemistry, and therefore be consistent with a bioreductionist model of psychosis.

The relationship between dissociation and psychosis cannot be a serious problem in the psychosis field until these definitional problems are resolved.

The Pseudohallucination Concept

The idea that some auditory hallucinations are *pseudo-hallucinations* is endorsed by both psychopharmacologists who treat schizophrenia and psychotherapists who treat dissociative disorders. However, there are no valid and reliable measures that can differentiate "true" from "pseudo" hallucinations. The differentiation exists only at the level of clinical folklore. According to my experience and observations, clinicians determine that a given auditory hallucination is either a "pseudo-hallucination" or a "true hallucination" after they have assigned the person to a category of psychosis or neurosis. Once the category is set, the decision about whether the hallucination is "true" or "pseudo" follows automatically.

This is a tautology, not a clinical determination. Psychopharmacologists who do not diagnose or treat dissociative disorders make diagnoses of schizophrenia or schizoaffective disorder and prescribe antipsychotic medications to individuals who subsequently receive psychotherapy for dissociative identity disorder. The auditory hallucinations that supported a diagnosis of schizophrenia are redefined as "pseudo" if the person is reassigned to the category of neurosis. However, this same symptom, in the same person, previously supported a diagnosis of psychosis when the person was deemed psychotic.

In order for dissociation to be taken seriously in the psychosis field, there needs to be a moratorium on use of the term *pseudo-hallucination*. The apparent conceptual order brought to the field by that term is tautological and illusory.

Problems with the DSM Criteria for Schizophrenia

According to the DSM-IV-TR diagnostic criteria for schizophrenia, only one positive symptom is required to make the diagnosis if there are voices talking to each other or commenting on the person's behavior. The other criteria deal with duration, impairment, and differential diagnosis. Schizophrenia, as defined in DSM-IV-TR, is really an *auditory hallucination disorder*, which is conceptually equivalent to *cough disorder* or *fever disorder*. Using a single symptom to define a severe and chronic disorder makes no sense medically, biologically, psychologically, or socially. The DSM-IV-TR diagnostic criteria for schizophrenia are guaranteed to capture a highly heterogeneous population with numerous different etiologies.

In fact, positive symptoms of schizophrenia, including auditory hallucinations, are more characteristic of dissociative identity disorder than of schizophrenia. Neither clinicians nor research measures can differentiate dissociative voices from psychotic voices. Indeed, persons with dissociative identity disorder score higher than persons with schizophrenia on measures like the Positive and Negative Syndrome

Scale (Kay, Opler, & Fiszbein, 1994), and psychosis subscales of the Symptom Checklist 90 (Derogatis, Lipman, Rickels, Uhenhuth, & Covi, 1973) and the Millon Clinical Multiaxial Inventory (Millon, 1977; Ross, 2004).

This is not surprising because Bleuler's (1950 [1911]) original description of schizophrenia was in fact a highly detailed description of dissociative identity disorder, at least for many of his cases. The reason he coined the term *schizophrenia,* which means *split mind,* was that he considered splitting of numerous psychic functions to be the central feature of the disorder. He also considered splitting to be synonymous with *dissociation.*

The psychological and physiological elements that can be dissociated in schizophrenia, according to Bleuler, include: attention, personality, touch, ideas, somatic sensations, will, memory, emotion, voice, hallucinations, movement, pain, arousal, personal name, and physiological functions (such as heart rate). Thus, dissociation was both pervasive and fundamental in Bleuler's view because it gave rise to virtually all the features of schizophrenia except for thought disorder. Bleuler's list of dissociative phenomena in schizophrenia was much broader than the DSM-IV-TR definition of dissociation as a "disruption in the usually integrated functions of consciousness, memory, identity or perception of the environment" (APA, 2000, p. 477).

Bleuler's schizophrenia includes the full range of psychoform dissociation measured by the Dissociative Experiences Scale (Bernstein & Putnam, 1986) and somatoform dissociation measured by the Somatoform Dissociation Questionnaire (Nijenhuis, 1999). Bleuler also noted frequent eating disorders in his caseload, which resembled the patients that Pierre Janet (1965 [1907]; 1977 [1901]) would diagnose as suffering from *hysteria.* Blueler's schizophrenia is more similar to Janet's hysteria and DSM-IV-TR's dissociative identity disorder than it is to DSM-IV-TR's schizophrenia.

Quotations from Bleuler's classic text, *Dementia Praecox or The Group of Schizophrenias* (1950 [1911]) make this point convincingly:

> In every case we are confronted with a more or less clear-cut splitting of psychic functions. If the disease is marked, the personality loses its unity; at different times different psychic complexes seem to represent the personality. Integration of different complexes and strivings appears insufficient or even lacking. The psychic complexes do not combine in a conglomeration of strivings with a unified resultant as they do in a healthy person; rather, one set of complexes dominates the personality for a time, while other

groups or drives are "split off" and seem either partly or completely impotent. (p. 9)

Since any part of the ego may be split off and, on the other hand, since entirely alien concepts may be attached to it, the patient may become "depersonalized." The person "loses his boundaries in time and space." The patients may identify themselves with some other person, even with inanimate objects, with a chair, with Switzerland. *Single emotionally charged ideas or drives attain a certain degree of autonomy so that the personality falls to pieces. These fragments can then exist side by side and alternately dominate the main part of the personality, the conscious part of the patient.* However, the patient may also become a definitely different person from a certain moment onwards. (p. 143, italics in original)

When the patients speak of themselves as different persons, they utilize a correspondingly different tone of voice. One of our patients spoke with the voice of the child who wanted to emerge through the patient's mouth.

When specific "persons" speak through the patients, in various cases of automatic speech, each "person" has his own special voice and distinct manner of speech. (p. 149)

Thus the person appears to be split into as many different persons or personalities as they have complexes. (p. 361)

Having provided this minutely detailed and thorough description of dissociative identity disorder, which he calls *schizophrenia*, Bleuler then claims that full splitting of the personality occurs only in his disease of schizophrenia, not in hysteria or multiple personality disorder. In DSM-IV-TR language, Bleuler is saying that Janet's patients have dissociative disorder not otherwise specified while his have dissociative identity disorder:

The systematic splitting, with reference to personality, for example, may be found in many other psychotic conditions; in hysteria they are even more marked than in schizophrenia (multiple personalities). Definite splitting, however, in the sense that various personality fragments exist side by side in a state of clear orientation as to environment, will only be found in our disease. (pp. 298-299)

To reiterate, what Bleuler calls *schizophrenia* is actually DSM-IV-TR dissociative identity disorder. What he calls hysteria or multiple personality disorder is actually DSM-IV-TR dissociative disorder not otherwise specified. This is why the diagnostic term *schizophrenia*, which means split mind, applies to schizophrenia but not, in Bleuler's view, to multiple personality disorder: the full splitting of the mind into dissociated persons occurs only in schizophrenia, of which multiple personality is a partial form.

Bleuler's text, by itself, provides overwhelming evidence that the relationship between dissociation and psychosis is complex and poorly understood in the schizophrenia field. One hundred years later, many people who meet DSM-IV-TR criteria for dissociative identity disorder still receive the diagnosis of schizophrenia from treating clinicians, and therefore receive antipsychotic medication but not intensive individual psychotherapy. False negative cases of DID contaminate the entire literature on schizophrenia including studies of phenomenology, biology, therapeutics, and genetics. Insisting that DID is rare and belongs to a discrete and separate category of peripheral interest does not solve the problem conceptually or clinically.

The relationship between dissociation and psychosis is important, in part, because there is such a high level of unrecognized dissociative symptoms in many people who are treated for schizophrenia. The diagnosis of schizophrenia can be made when the only symptom is a voice or voices talking inside the person's mind, but these voices can, in principle, be caused by trauma and treated with psychotherapy. The DSM-IV-TR diagnostic criteria for schizophrenia are incapable of scientifically assigning a person to the category of psychosis because the same symptoms can be symptoms of neurosis. The DSM-IV-TR criteria for schizophrenia generate many false positives of schizophrenia and many false negatives of dissociative identity disorder.

Problems with Research Measures

As mentioned above, research measures cannot differentiate dissociation and psychosis. For instance, auditory hallucinations are asked about by both the Dissociative Experiences Scale and the Positive and Negative Syndrome Scale (Pincus, Rush, First, & McQueen, 2000). Determining whether an auditory hallucination is dissociative or psychotic in nature is a problem with both definitions and measures. This applies not just to voices, but to the full range of Schneiderian symptoms including: made thoughts, feelings and actions; thought insertion and withdrawal; and thoughts ascribed to others. All these can occur due to intrusions into the executive self from dissociated part selves, or, in principle, can be due to biological brain disease.

Problems in the Sociology of Psychiatry

The problems discussed above are simultaneously problems in the sociology of psychiatry. The field of psychiatry is composed of dissociated subsystems that do not communicate or cooperate with each other. One subsystem is a set of experts (all with MD's and PhD's), journals, grant agencies, appointments, and diagnoses and treatments gathered under the heading of "biological psychiatry." This subsystem is highly subsidized by the pharmaceutical industry, and has control of academic psychiatry, in terms of appointments, promotions, grants, publishing, invitations to speak at conferences at Department of Psychiatry Grand Rounds, and at other functions.

A second subsystem consists of a large number of Master's level psychotherapists, supplemented by MD's and PhD's, who do not have academic appointments, grants, extensive publications, or influence in academia. This is the dissociative disorders field. The dissociative disorders field has virtually no support from drug companies, few research grants, and very little influence in academia. These sociological characteristics of the dissociation and psychosis fields must change in order for dissociation to be integrated into serious, mainstream study of schizophrenia and related disorders.

Problems with the Drug Industry

There is no medication for dissociation. Therefore, the dissociative disorders are "orphan" disorders from the perspective of the pharmaceutical industry. They do not warrant funding or investigation because there is no potential profit to offset the costs of conducting drug trials for dissociative disorders. Individuals with dissociative disorders are regularly prescribed antidepressants, antipsychotics, anxiolytics, and mood stabilizers under "off label" prescribing practices.

"Off-label indication" means that a medication is being prescribed for a diagnosis that has not been officially approved by the Food and Drug Administration. An example would be prescribing an antipsychotic medication to a child with attention deficit disorder. Until drug companies are convinced that trials of medications for dissociation make financial sense, there is no reason for them to pursue anything other than off-label prescribing for dissociative disorders. Until this situation changes, the relationship between dissociation and psychosis will not receive adequate time, attention, energy and resources from academic psychiatry. This is so because drug company interests have a pervasive influence on conceptual models,

diagnostic practices, research agendas, and treatment protocols in psychiatry. The ideology of biological brain disease-drug treatment controls psychiatry and is massively reinforced financially by the pharmaceutical
industry. Other models and therapies are all orphans by default.

Assumptions About Etiology

The different categories of conceptual problems concerning dissociation and psychosis overlap a great deal. As mentioned above, despite lip
service paid to the biopsychosocial model, the prevailing assumption in
psychiatry is the belief that psychosis is caused by brain disease. Psychosis is a symptom of disordered biology. Dissociation, in comparison, is viewed as "soft," non-medical, ephemeral, and "reactive." Until
these assumptions about etiology are changed, dissociation will not be
taken seriously in the psychosis field.

Assumptions About Treatment

Assumptions about treatment follow from assumptions about etiology. In North American academic psychiatry, individual psychotherapy
for schizophrenia virtually does not exist. In the rare case that it is prescribed, psychotherapy is adjunctive and directed at adjustment and
general coping. The idea that individual psychotherapy could be the primary treatment for schizophrenia receives no serious consideration.

Until a balanced biopsychosocial model is adopted in mainstream
psychiatry, there will be no reason to consider dissociation seriously in
diagnosis and treatment of schizophrenia. Within biological psychiatry,
psychotherapy for schizophrenia makes no more sense than psychotherapy for lung cancer.

For psychotherapy to be prescribed often, the diagnosis must be
switched to a category that permits it. For instance, schizophrenia will
become schizoaffective disorder, and schizoaffective disorder will become rapid cycling bipolar mood disorder, which in turn will become
borderline personality disorder, until finally, a therapist realizes that the
correct diagnosis is dissociative identity disorder. Now psychotherapy
can be prescribed and antipsychotic medications will be adjunctive.
During this period of time, neither the biology nor the psychology of the
person receiving services has changed. These adjustments to diagnosis
and treatment are also regularly made in the opposite direction.

RECOMMENDATIONS

For the above conceptual problems to be solved there has to be a thorough restructuring of the mental health field, a paradigm shift. Although one may be in process, it is moving very slowly at best. In the twenty-seven years since I diagnosed my first case of multiple personality disorder in 1979 (Ross, 1984), I have seen at most only a minute shift in mainstream academia towards a trauma-dissociation model of schizophrenia.

Given the slow pace of conceptual change in psychiatry, what are some realistic, attainable goals in the time frame of the DSM-V, which should be published in 2010 or 2011, and the DSM-VI, which should presumably be published about ten years later?

A Truly Biopsychosocial Model

Due to recent discoveries in the normal biology of mammalian response to stress, it is now possible that a new model of mind-brain interaction may be adopted in psychiatry. Stress-induced, high levels of cortisol cause damage and death to hippocampal neurons (Sapolsky, 2000), which can be repaired and replaced. Repair and replacement of neurons was thought to be impossible when I was in medical school in 1979. However, it appears that repair of damaged hippocampal neurons can be augmented by psychiatric medications including mood stabilizers and selective serotonin reuptake inhibitor antidepressants (McDonald et al., 2006). Only one additional fact remains to be established: that psychotherapy can also promote hippocampal self-repair. If this is demonstrated within the next decade, we will then have scientific proof of a sequence of events: psychological trauma can damage the brain; this is a genetically normal mammalian response; and the damage can be repaired through psychotherapy.

A unidirectional bioreductionist model could not account for these facts. For brain self-repair to be initiated and carried out through psychotherapy, causality would have to run in two directions: brain to mind, and mind to brain. This would be a truly biopsychosocial model of mental disorders, and dissociation would be at its core (Ross, 2000; 2004) because dissociation is a core component of the trauma response. Hippocampal damage would be expected to cause failures in the normal integration of consciousness, identity, feeling, and sensation–that is, expected to cause dissociative symptoms.

I assume that antidepressants and psychotherapy will prove to have a synergistic effect on hippocampal repair. Effort should be expended to gather the necessary psychotherapy outcome data to support this paradigm shift. I predict that once the shift has occurred, trauma-induced dissociation will be just as "biological" as psychosis, and psychosis will be just as "psychological" as dissociation, because psychotic symptoms will also respond to the psychotherapy protocols that treat dissociation.

Diagnostic and Statistical Manual of Mental Disorders (5th ed.) (DSM-V)

There is not enough time to generate all the data required for a thorough restructuring of DSM-V. Therefore, efforts should focus on having the high frequency of dissociative symptoms in schizophrenia recognized in DSM-V. This could occur in the text in both the general discussion and the section on differential diagnosis. Dissociative symptoms could also be recognized in a dissociative subtype of schizophrenia (Ross, 1994), characterized by auditory hallucinations, amnesia and depersonalization, extensive comoridity and childhood trauma. DSM-V literature reviews and field studies should address the role of dissociation in schizophrenia and other psychoses.

Research Designs

Research studies of psychosis should include measures of childhood trauma and dissociation. The Dissociative Experiences Scale is a 28-item self-report measure that has an extensive data-base and well-studied psychometric properties (Pincus et al., 2000). It could easily be incorporated into studies of the phenomenology, epidemiology, biology, and treatment of psychosis. According to my theory, the dissociative subtype of schizophrenia has a set of characteristics that include: more psychobiology of trauma; less psychobiology of endogenous subtypes of schizophrenia; poorer response to D2-receptor antipsychotic medications; better response to psychotherapy; more comorbidity on Axis I and II; and higher risk for oculogyric crises and tardive dykinesia.

Further studies of psychotic symptoms should also be undertaken for populations in treatment for dissociative disorders because the relationship is bi-directional: A subgroup of dissociative disorders has more psychotic symptoms; and a subset of psychoses has more dissociative symptoms. These two subgroups resemble each other more than either resembles non-dissociative psychoses or non-psychotic dissociative disorders. Here I am using the terms "psychotic" and "dissociative" in their operational meaning–the symptoms defined by various measures.

This discussion is not intended to be exhaustive or fully referenced. My goal has been to outline some key conceptual issues in the relationship between dissociation and psychosis. More complete argument, evidence and references are available elsewhere (Ross, 2004).

REFERENCES

American Psychiatric Association. (2000). *Diagnostic and statistical manual of mental disorders (4th ed., text revision).* Washington, DC: Author.

Bernstein, E. M., & Putnam, F. W. (1986). Development, reliability, and validity of a dissociation scale. *Journal of Nervous and Mental Disease, 174,* 727-735.

Bleuler, E. (1950). *Dementia praecox or the group of schizophrenias.* In J. Zinkin (Trans.). The schizophrenic disorders: Long term patient and family studies. New York: International Universities Press. (Original work published 1911)

Carter, C. S. (2006). Understanding the glass ceiling for functional outcome in schizophrenia. *American Journal of Psychiatry, 163,* 356-358.

Derogatis, L. R., Lipman, R. S., Rickels, K., Uhenhuth, E. H., & Covi, L. (1973). SCL-90: An outpatient psychiatric rating scale–preliminary reports. *Psychopharmacology Bulletin, 9,* 13-28.

Janet, P. (1965). *The major symptoms of hysteria.* New York: Hafner. (Original work published 1907)

Janet, P. (1977). *The mental state of hystericals.* Washington, DC: University Publications of America. (Original work published 1901)

Kay, S. R., Opler, L. A., & Fiszbein, A. (1994). *Positive and negative syndrome manual.* North Tonawanda, NY: Multi-Health Systems.

Keith, S. J. (2006). Are we still talking to our patients with schizophrenia? *American Journal of Psychiatry, 163,* 362364.

McDonald, C., Marshall, N., Sham, P.C., Bullmore, E.T., Schulze, K., Chapple, B., et al., (2006). Regional brain morphometry in patients with schizophrenia or bipolar disorder and their unaffected relatives. *American Journal of Psychiatry, 163,* 478-487.

Millon, T. (1977). *Millon clinical multiaxial inventory manual.* Minneapolis: National Computer Systems.

Nijenhuis, E. R. S. (1999). *Somatoform dissociation: Phenomena, measurement, and theoretical issues.* Assen, The Netherlans: Van Gorcum.

Onitsuka, T., Niznikiewicz, M. A., Spencer, K. M., Frimin, M., Kuroki, N., Lucia, L. C., Shenton, M. E., & McCarley, R. W. (2006). Functional and structural deficits in brain regions subserving face perception in schizophrenia. *American Journal of Psychiatry, 163,* 455-462.

Pincus, H. A., Rush, A. J., First, M. B., & McQueen, L. E. (2000). Handbook of psychiatric measures. Washington, DC: American Psychiatric Association.

Read, J., Mosher, L. R., & Bentall, R. P. (2004). *Models of madness: Psychological, social and biological approaches to schizophrenia.* New York:Brunner-Routledge.

Ross, C. A. (1984). Diagnosis of multiple personality during hypnosis: A case report. *International Journal of Clinical and Experimental Hypnosis, 32,* 222-235.

Ross, C. A. (1994). *The Osiris complex: Case studies in multiple personality.* Toronto, Canada: University of Toronto Press.

Ross, C. A. (2000). *The trauma model: A solution to the problem of comorbidity in Psychiatry.* Richardson, TX: Manitou Communications, Inc.

Ross, C. A. (2004). *Schizophrenia: Innovations in diagnosis and treatment.* New York: The Haworth Press, Inc.

Sapolsky, R. M. (2000). Glucocorticoids and hippocampal atrophy in neuropsychiatric disorders. *Archives of General Psychiatry, 57,* 925-935.

Turkington, D., Kingdon, D., & Weiden, P. J. (2006). Cognitive behavior therapy for schizophrenia. *American Journal of Psychiatry, 163,* 365-373.

doi:10.1300/J513v06n02_03

Auditory Hallucinations: Psychotic Symptom or Dissociative Experience?

Andrew Moskowitz
Dirk Corstens

SUMMARY. While auditory hallucinations are considered a core psychotic symptom, central to the diagnosis of schizophrenia, it has long been recognized that persons who are not psychotic may also hear voices. There is an entrenched clinical belief that distinctions can be made between these groups, typically, on the basis of the perceived location or the 'third-person' perspective of the voices. While it is generally believed that such characteristics of voices have significant clinical implications, and are important in the differential diagnosis between dissociative and psychotic disorders, there is no research evidence in support of this. Voices heard by persons diagnosed schizophrenic appear to be indistinguishable, on the basis of their experienced characteristics,

Andrew Moskowitz, PhD, is affiliated with the University of Aberdeen, Department of Mental Health, Institute of Medical Science, Foresterhill, Aberdeen, Scotland.

Dirk Corstens is Psychiatrist and Cognitive Therapist, Social Psychiatric Service Riagg Maastricht, Maastricht, The Netherlands.

Please address correspondence to: Andrew Moskowitz, PhD, University of Aberdeen, Department of Mental Health, Institute of Medical Science, Foresterhill, Aberdeen, AB25 2ZD, Scotland, United Kingdom (E-mail: a.moskowitz@abdn.ac.uk).

[Haworth co-indexing entry note]: "Auditory Hallucinations: Psychotic Symptom or Dissociative Experience?" Moskowitz, Andrew, and Dirk Corstens. Co-published simultaneously in *Journal of Psychological Trauma* (The Haworth Maltreatment & Trauma Press, an imprint of The Haworth Press) Vol. 6, No. 2/3, 2007, pp. 35-63; and: *Trauma and Serious Mental Illness* (ed: Steven N. Gold, and Jon D. Elhai) The Haworth Maltreatment & Trauma Press, an imprint of The Haworth Press, 2007, pp. 35-63. Single or multiple copies of this article are available for a fee from The Haworth Document Delivery Service [1-800-HAWORTH, 9:00 a.m. - 5:00 p.m. (EST). E-mail address: docdelivery@haworthpress.com].

Available online at http://jpsyt.haworthpress.com
doi:10.1300/J513v06n02_04

from voices heard by persons with dissociative disorders or by persons with no mental disorder at all. On this and other bases outlined in this article, we argue that hearing voices should be considered a dissociative experience, which under some conditions may have pathological consequences. In other words, we believe that, while voices may occur in the context of a psychotic disorder, they should not be considered a psychotic symptom. doi:10.1300/J513v06n02_04 *[Article copies available for a fee from The Haworth Document Delivery Service: 1-800-HAWORTH. E-mail address: <docdelivery@haworthpress.com> Website: <http://www.HaworthPress.com>* © 2007 by The Haworth Press, Inc. All rights reserved.]*

KEYWORDS. Auditory hallucinations, dissociation, psychosis, diagnosis

"Once you hear the voices, you realize they've always been there. It's just a matter of being tuned to them."

(Mark Vonnegut, *The Eden Express*, 1975)

Mark Vonnegut's simple insight, expressed in his compelling autobiographical account of becoming psychotic in America in the 1960s, supports the position put forth in this paper. Namely, that hearing voices should be considered a dissociative experience and not a psychotic symptom. This position is opposed to that of most clinicians and researchers, who believe that auditory hallucinations[1] (AH) are best considered a psychotic symptom, or that some AH should be considered psychotic and others dissociative. Nonetheless, our position is supported by both clinical and research evidence, including the fact that many persons who hear voices do not show any (other) symptom of a mental disorder, and that no experienced characteristic of voices adequately distinguishes between those persons and others who are designated mentally ill. Accordingly, we propose that AH should, under no circumstances, be considered a psychotic symptom, despite the fact that they sometimes occur in the context of a psychotic disorder.

Throughout recorded history, AH have been understood in a number of ways. At various times, and under various circumstances, voices have been viewed as religious or spiritual phenomena (voices of gods, demons, angels), supernatural or psychic experiences (indicative of ghosts or telepathy), psychological experiences (post-traumatic, dissociative, psychotic), or entirely normal (voice of conscience, one's own thoughts, creative inspiration, grief experiences, hypnopompic, and hypnagogic experiences). Over the past 150 years, considerable effort has been expended in attempting to distinguish between these allegedly different forms of hallucinations, particularly along the lines of determining which voices merit the attention of physicians or mental health professionals and which do not.

Typically, these attempts have been mounted around certain perceived characteristics of auditory hallucinations, most commonly, whether the voices appear to be emanating from outside the voice hearer or from inside their head (or some other part of their body). Classically, the latter, particularly when combined with 'intact' insight, have been referred to as 'pseudo-hallucinations,' while only the former, i.e., 'external' hallucinations, have been accorded the label 'proper hallucinations' or 'true hallucinations' and considered a psychotic symptom (Jaspers, 1963/1913). However, insight is technically not an experienced aspect of the hallucination but a subsequent evaluation by the voice hearer (essentially equivalent to a secondary delusion). While it appears likely that there are some–as yet unidentified–personality or psychological factors which determine whether voices are heard internally or externally (and help to explain why one person can hear both internal and external voices and why some voices' perceived source of location may change), there is no evidence that perceived location (or any other experienced characteristic of AH) map onto diagnostic categories or relevant clinical variables (such as treatment response). Indeed, a recent study pointedly titled 'On the non-significance of internal versus external auditory hallucinations' examined this issue in a large cohort and concluded, "(T)he clinical relevance of location is not confirmed, and the conceptual clarity and clinical utility of the pseudohallucination is undermined" (Copolov, Trauer, & Mackinnon, 2004, p. 5).

Berrios and Dening (1996), in an exhaustive historical review, likened the concept of 'pseudohallucinations' to a "'joker' in the diagnostic game" whose fluidity allowed clinicians to "call into question the genuineness of some true hallucinatory experiences that do not fit into a pre-conceived psychiatric diagnosis" (p. 761).

If this is so–if there is no reliable way to distinguish hallucinations experienced in persons diagnosed with schizophrenia from those with other disorders or even from the general non-psychiatric population–what then do we make of auditory hallucinations?[2] While AH have long been considered a core symptom of psychosis, if their clinical utility remains limited, should that assumption be re-evaluated? Should the concept of auditory hallucinations be decoupled from the concept of psychosis? And if that occurs, what becomes of the concept of psychosis?

HISTORICAL OVERVIEW

Why some people do and others do not hear voices, and how to understand those voices, has been the subject of debate throughout the centuries. The two questions are closely related, as assumptions about voices have usually (but not always) been made by persons who do not hear voices, and their judgments have often been strongly colored by class, gender, and race beliefs. But was there a time when hearing voices was considered entirely normal? While the research data reviewed below suggests, currently, as many as 8-10% of the general population hear voices at some point in their life, one theorist believes that, millennia ago, *all* people heard voices. Julian Jaynes (1976), in a popular and controversial book, has argued that, until a few thousand years ago, humans did not possess self-reflective consciousness, and heard voices they attributed to gods, which guided their decision-making in small and large matters. He called this ancient mental structure the 'bicameral' mind, and argued that people who hear voices in modern times experience a relapse to this form of mind, primarily under the influence of extreme stress. Jaynes also predicted that hearing voices would be associated with activity in the right temporal lobe, analogous to the left hemisphere speech recognition/understanding center known as Wernicke's area. While Jayne's highly speculative theory has received little attention in psychiatric circles, there is now some evidence, reviewed below, in support of his contentions.

For much of recorded human history, hearing voices was associated with divine inspiration, or Satanic possession; as such, those who decided the source of others' voices (often on nebulous criteria) were typically associated with the Christian Church or other religions (Sarbin & Juhasz, 1967). Then, in the mid 16th century, Teresa of Avila, fearful that her nuns would be persecuted by the Inquisition for the voices they heard, argued that some voices should not be seen as divine or devilish, but as the result of more mundane physical problems. She wrote that some voices were due to melancholy, a 'weak' imagination, or drowsiness, sleep, or sleep-like states (Sarbin & Juhasz, 1967). Importantly, Teresa wrote that such individuals should be treated 'as if' they were sick, but Sarbin and Juhasz note that the 'as if' was quickly dropped as the phenomenon of hearing voices became medicalized.

The medical perspective became the dominant mode of understanding hallucinations (in all sensory modalities) in the 19th century, a term given its modern definition by Esquirol in 1832. Esquirol distinguished hallucinations from illusions on the basis that the latter involved genuine sensory perceptions (plus distortions); he stated that a person hallucinating "ascribes a body and an actuality to images that the memory recalls without intervention of the senses" (Esquirol, 1832, cited in Bentall, 1990, p. 82). While Esquirol believed that hallucinations were invariably pathological, a dispute developed in subsequent decades as to whether this was so.

This question culminated in a series of debates at the *Société Médico-Psychologique* in Paris, foreshadowing many of the debates still held today. As summarized by Berrios and Dening (1996), these discussions considered "whether all hallucinations were abnormal; and whether location (internal *versus* external) and insight (present *versus* absent) were relevant factors to the definition of pathological hallucinations" (p. 756). Berrios and Dening (1996) note that these important debates were overlooked by Karl Jaspers, in his highly influential *General Psychopathology* (1963/1913), who attributed the distinctions to an important figure from the 1880s: Victor Kandinsky.

Kandinsky (Table 1) was important not only because, unlike the French theorists, he himself experienced hallucinations, but also because he claimed to experience both 'true' (TH) and 'pseudo' (PH) hallucinations, and endeavored to distinguish between the two[3]. Kandinsky argued that only TH involved the activity of a subcortical perception center (just like genuine perceptions), while PH involved only the activity of a center for apperception (a term rarely used now, which means the state of being conscious of perceiving) along with a 'center for abstract, unconscious images' (Berrios & Dening, 1996). Thus, Kandinsky decided that PH were as sensorially vivid as TH, but lacked the 'external objectivity' of TH because in only the latter was the subcortical perception center activitated. He also believed that PH were internally localized.

Building on Kandinsky's distinctions, Jaspers (1963/1913) developed a concept of PH which was dominant throughout the 20th century. Jaspers claimed that PH were similar to TH in that they both had 'full, fresh sensory elements' and could not be voluntarily controlled, but differed from the latter in that they were experienced in 'inner subjective space' and did not appear concretely real. Admittedly, Jaspers concept of 'reality' here is vague and has led to differing interpretations.

Jaspers' view of PH held sway for half a century, until a series of papers out of Britain began to reconsider the concept. In three papers published in 1966, Sedman (1966a, 1966b, 1966c), on the basis of phenomenological research, rejected the equation of PH with 'inner' voices, arguing that location was irrelevant, but that PH were 'ego-syn-

TABLE 1. Historical Conceptions of Auditory 'Pseudo' (PH) and 'True' (TH) Hallucinations

Author	Pseudo-hallucinations (PH)	True hallucinations (TH)	Diagnostic associations
Kandinsky (1885)	- very vivid but less 'objectively real' than perceptions - internally localized	- very vivid and as 'objectively real' as perceptions - externally localized	
Jaspers (1913)	- lacked 'concrete reality' - perceived in 'inner subjective space'	- as real as perceptions - perceived in 'external' subjective space	
Sedman (1966)	- ego-syntonic - lack 'publicness' (i.e., not expected to be heard by others)	- ego-dystonic - perceived as public (i.e., expected to be heard by others)	TH associated with schizophrenia PH associated with hysterical and obsessive traits
Hare (1973)	AH with intact insight in psychiatric patients	AH without insight (interpreted delusionally) in psychiatric patients	TH associated with schizophrenia PH associated with "depressive psychosis, obsessional states or histrionic behavior"

tonic' and lacked 'publicness' (i.e., the person did not expect the voice to be heard by others), while TH were 'ego-dystonic' and perceived as public phenomena. However, echoing Jaspers, he claimed that TH were exclusively related to schizophrenia or schizoaffective disorder. Hare (1973) went further, arguing, somewhat tautologically, that any voices heard by non-psychiatric patients should be considered non-pathological, and that the term PH should be reserved for voices heard by psychiatric patients but interpreted non-delusionally (i.e., a voice of conscience, hearing one's thoughts). TH were all voices experienced by psychiatric patients and interpreted delusionally. Finally, Taylor (1981) attempted to bring some clarity to the discussion by suggesting that PH had been used in two different ways over the past 100 years, one, which he called 'imaged' PH, linked more to German authors and the other, which he called 'perceptual' PH, linked to British authors. The key difference, Taylor (1981) suggested, was that imaged PH, as propounded by Kandinsky and Jaspers, involved imagery, not perceptions, described as being less vivid and 'real' than TH, and internally localized, while perceptual PH, as propounded by Sedman and Hare, were not phenomenologically different from TH, but were accompanied by intact insight, in contrast to the latter. Taylor did not endorse one approach over the other, but insisted that authors should be clear as to which definition they were using.

This entire history has been thoroughly reviewed by Berrios and Dening (1996), who as noted above, strongly questioned the validity of the concept of pseudohallucinations. However, in a parallel paper, Dening and Berrios (1996) argued that many clinicians continue to believe that not all hallucinations have the same clinical import. This desire to 'separate out' some forms of AH from others can be clearly seen in the various 20th century attempts to 'parse out' hallucinations and relate them to different conditions and diagnoses.

AUDITORY HALLUCINATIONS AND DIFFERENTIAL DIAGNOSIS

Auditory hallucinations were not central features of either Kraepelin's *Dementia Praecox* or Bleuler's *Schizophrenia*. For Bleuler, AH, while occurring frequently in schizophrenia, were derivative of the central disturbance of loosening of associations, and were also common in other disorders. A much closer link between AH and schizophrenia, however, was forged by Kurt Schneider (1959), whose position underpins the diagnosis of schizophrenia in the DSM-IV (American Psychiatric Association, 1994) and ICD-10 (WHO, 1993). Schneider felt that certain AH, particularly those commenting on an individual's thoughts or behaviors or two or more voices conversing with each other, were pathognomic (only one symptom required for a diagnosis) for schizophrenia; he also thought that hearing one's thoughts aloud was characteristic of the disorder. The first two symptoms were adopted by the American Psychiatric Association for the diagnosis of schizophrenia, and now form two of the three pathognomic symptoms (the third, also problematic, is 'bizarre' delusions[4]). Interestingly, while the American Psychiatric Association (APA) had specifically linked external AH to schizophrenia in early DSMs, this link was eliminated (presumably for lack of empirical evidence) in the DSM-IV (APA, 1994).

There is, however, considerable evidence that AH, *particularly* those considered pathognomic for schizophrenia, are not only *not* unique to that disorder but occur *more* frequently in dissociative identity disorder (Honig, Romme, Ensink, Escher, Pennings, & deVries, 1998; Kluft, 1987; Ross, Heber, Norton, & Anderson, 1989; Ross, Miller, Reagor, Bjornson, & Fraser, 1990). In light of this observation, several authors have argued for new dissociative diagnostic categories ('Dissociative hallucinosis,' Nurcombe, Mitchell, Begtrup, Tramontana, LaBarbera, & Pruitt, 1996; 'Dissociative subtype of schizophrenia,' Ross, 2004) in which AH are featured prominently.

Other authors have taken a different tack, addressing AH directly by proposing new classificatory systems. Thus, Van der Zwaard and Polak (2001), after reviewing the concept of pseudohallucinations, argue that PH should be broken up into several categories, namely: (a) nonpsychotic hallucinations (e.g., 'isolated' nonpsychotic hallucinations, such as occur in grief reactions, AH arising from sensory deprivation, and 'vivid internal imagery,' typical in dissociative disorders), (b) partial hallucinations, such as 'fading hallucinations with increasing insight,' and (c) transient hallucinations (such as 'short lapses' in reality testing in persons diagnosed with borderline personality disorder). This classification appears to offer little improvement over the simply PH/TH dichotomy; it seems difficult to justify calling AH in dissociative disorders 'imagery' and 'partial hallucinations' appears to be a nonsensical concept. Further, there is evidence that AH in borderline personality disorder are not transient, as has been generally believed, but in fact are 'ongoing and pervasive' (Yee et al., 2005). In light of this, Yee et al (2005) has offered an alternative classification, namely that AH be split up into: (a) normative, (b) traumatic-intrusive, (c) psychotic, and (d) organic hallucinations. But is there any evidence that AH can be successfully carved up in this (or any other) manner?

RESEARCH EVIDENCE

A number of relevant research studies have now been conducted, examining the prevalence of hallucinations in the general population, contrasting voices heard by patients with non-patients or, within clinical populations, assessing whether certain characteristics of voices predict clinical or outcome variables. Some studies have also demonstrated clear links between AH and dissociative experiences.

AH in non-psychiatric patients. The studies assessing the prevalence and nature of auditory hallucinations in non-psychiatric populations are illustrated in Table 2.

Six large-scale studies, based primarily in the UK, the Netherlands, and the U.S., have found rates of between 0.6% to 8.2% annual or lifetime prevalence of hallucinations in the general population (excluding, to a greater or lesser degree, identified psychiatric patients)[5]. Three studies of selected non-psychiatric samples, primarily university students or medical patients, have reported slightly higher rates, ranging from 2%-13%.

The first large-scale study to assess hallucinations in the general population was carried out primarily in England between 1889 and 1892, and involved interviews with 17,000 adults (Sidgewick et al., 1894). This study, known as the Sidgewick study after the first author, was conducted by the Society for Psychical Research (SPR), an organization dedicated to researching psychic phenomena, such as telepathy. As such, a number of the interviewers may have been biased toward discovering hallucinations in non-psychiatric patients. However, the study has been described as well designed, and incorporated a number of relevant exclusion criteria (Tien, 1991). Sidgewick and colleagues found approximately 10% of their participants to have experienced visual, auditory, or tactile hallucinations over their lifetime, just under 7% when corrected for sleep-related experiences. Most of those hallucinations were visual. Those experiencing auditory hallucinations decreased from 2% of those in their 20s, to just under 1% for those over 30. In addition, a gender bias was recorded, with women experiencing more hallucinations than men.

The results of the Sidgewick study were broadly similar to those found in a large-scale US study 90 years later. The NIMH Epidemiological Catchment Area (ECA) project took place in the early 1980s, and involved structured interviews with over 18,000 adults in five major metropolitan areas (Tien, 1991). While the lifetime prevalence for any hallucination was slightly higher in the ECA study–13%–this figure,

TABLE 2. Prevalence of AH in the General Population

Study	Country	n	experiencing AH[1]	AH <u>and</u> clinically distressed or psychiatrically involved
Sidgewick (1894)	UK[2]	15,316	1-2%[3]	-
Posey & Losch (1983-1984)	USA	375 students	~10%	-
ECA (Tien, 1991)	USA	15,258	2-3%[3]	~33%
Barrett & Etheridge (1992)	USA	585 students	6-13%[4]	-
Van Os et al (2000)	Holland	7076	~8%[5]	22%
Ohayon (2000)	Germany, Italy, UK	13,057	0.6%	-
Johns et al (2002)	UK	8063	0.6-3%[6]	25%
Dhossche et al (2002)	Holland	914 adolescents	5%	-
Glicksohn & Barrett (2003)	Israel	656 students	2-9%[4]	-

[1] Excluding sleep-related, hearing one's name, or one's own thoughts aloud, where indicated.
[2] Plus a small percentage in Russia and Brazil.
[3] Varies with age group.
[4] Percentage endorsing one of a series of AH questions.
[5] A small percentage of the reported hallucinations may have been non-auditory.
[6] Varies with ethnic group. Highest in 'Caribbean' sample, lowest in 'Asian' sample.

which also included olfactory and gustatory hallucinations, did not significantly differ from the Sidgewick result. Across the age groups, auditory hallucinations averaged about 2% lifetime prevalence, with the exception of 18-19 year olds, 3% of whom endorsed such experiences.

Importantly, while the ECA study was designed to assess the prevalence of mental disorders in the community, the majority of those endorsing auditory hallucinations did not appear to be mentally ill, as most claimed that these experiences were not a cause of distress or led to any impairment in their functioning.

Interest in this area has accelerated over the past few years, with four groups of researchers publishing population-based study results since 2000. Jim van Os and his colleagues (2000) in the Netherlands assessed a random sample of over 7000 adults, finding a lifetime prevalence of 8.2% for hallucinations (primarily auditory); as in the ECA study, the vast majority of those who responded positively reported that they were not bothered by their hallucinations and had not sought treatment for them.

In a UK study, over 8000 individuals were screened for mental health problems as part of the Fourth National Survey of Ethnic Minorities (Johns, Nazroo, Bebbington, & Kuipers, 2002). One question on the screening was about hearing voices saying "quite a few words or sentences when there was no one around that might account for it." While just over 1% of the 'white' sample responded affirmatively to this question, almost 3% of the 'Caribbean' sample did likewise (but only 0.6% of the Asian group). The figures represent annual prevalence rates. Again, only 25% of this group met criteria for a psychotic disorder when further assessed (by telephone), and there was no relation between a reported history of diagnosis or treatment for psychosis and hearing voices. This is particularly notable as hearing, "quite a few words or sentences" reflects a fairly high level of AH (Posey & Losch, 1983).

Similar results were found in a Dutch study of 914 adolescents (Dhossche, Ferdinand, Van der Ende, Hofstra, & Verhulst, 2002) who were followed up eight years later (86% of initial cohort successfully contacted). Five percent of the initial cohort, and two percent of those followed-up, endorsed AH on a self-report questionnaire. While AH were associated with depressive and substance abuse disorders (determined by a structured interview), there was no statistical association with any psychotic disorder.

Finally, one study did find a link between AH and psychotic diagnoses in the community (Ohayon, 2000). This study involved telephone interviewing of over 13,000 persons aged 15 or older in the UK, Germany, and Italy, using an instrument designed to assess sleep-related disorders and experiences. Non-sleep-related AH, found in 0.6% of the participants, were considerably less common than in the prior studies.

Participants who heard voices at least once a week had significantly higher levels of psychotic and depressive disorders, but the strongest associations were with anxiety and bipolar disorders. However, this was not true for persons hearing daytime voices on a less than once a month basis. The lower levels of population-based AH in this study may have been due to methodological issues, including the use of telephone interviews, an instrument not primarily designed to assess psychiatric disorders or symptoms, and an inflexible interview schedule.

Three studies, also displayed in Table 2, have found auditory hallucinations to be commonly experienced by university students. In Posey and Losch's (1983) study, close to 10% of 375 students reported hearing a "comforting or advising" voice and 5% reported conducting conversations with the voice(s). The authors concluded that "clinical finding of hallucinations of a mild sort . . . should not be taken as suggestive of psychopathology" (p. 111).

Barrett and Etheridge (1992) replicated Posey and Losch's (1983) study, with a larger sample (at the same university). Between 6.1% and 12.6% of the sample endorsed hearing voices that were not (apparently) their thoughts, their name being called, or sleep-related. Barrett and Etheridge did not report on percentages of participants conversing with their voices. Importantly, they also found that psychopathology, as rated by either the MMPI (Hathaway & McKinley, 1967) or the SCL-90-R (Derogatis, 1994) was unrelated to AH. Echoing Posey and Losch, they concluded, "Reports of verbal hallucinations in the general population cannot reasonably be explained as the result of psychopathology" (Barrett & Etheridge, 1992, p. 385).

Further evidence of the frequency of hallucinations in student populations was provided by a research study of over 600, primarily Israeli, university students, conducted by Joseph Glicksohn and Barrett (2003). Using a modification of the Barrett and Etheridge (1992) measure, they found between two and nine percent of their sample endorsing AH consistent with those endorsed by students in previous studies. But are these AH similar to those experienced by psychiatric patients, or can they be characterized as 'pseudo-hallucinations' and distinguished from the hallucinations of psychiatric patients?

PHENOMENOLOGY AND CLINICAL UTILITY

As was noted in the historical overview of this topic, the feature of AH most often put forth as central to distinguishing 'true' from 'pseudo' hallucinations is the perceived location of the voice. While recent reviews have criticized this position, many in the psychiatric field continue to believe that external voices are characteristic of psychotic AH, and internal voices indicative of dissociative or 'normal' voices. There has now been a number of studies which have addressed this issue, the results of which can be seen in Table 3. While most of the studies include only psychiatric patients, two directly compare the AH of psychiatric patients with those of non-patients.

A cursory glance at the table offers little support for the clinical adage described above. While between 31% and 61% of persons diagnosed schizophrenic hear exclusively external voices, 56% of non-schizophrenic psychiatric patients, 27% of those with dissociative disorders, and 40% of non-patients do as well. The medical patients in Mott, Small, and Anderson's (1965) study are not considered here for reasons described in the table). Exclusively internal voices are reported by 22-43% of those diagnosed schizophrenic, 31% of those with psychotic diagnoses other than schizophrenia, 33% of those with dissociative disorders, and 47% of non-patients. The most significant variation occurs in the percentage of psychiatric patients reported to hear both internal and external voices, which varies between 6% and 42%; however, it appears likely that at least some of this variation can be attributed to methodological issues.

Thus, while the AH of psychiatric patients and non-patients do not appear to be different with regard to perceived location, there are differences in the relationship and reaction to the voices. Honig and colleagues (1998) reported that non-patients heard fewer 'negative' voices than both sets of patients (53% compared to 93% and 100%), but all groups heard high levels of positive voices. The most significant differences related to responses to the voices–more than 3/4 of the patients were afraid of the voices, but none of the non-patients (NP) was. Likewise, all of the patients, but only 20% of the non-patients, reported that the voices disturbed their daily life, and all of the NP but only 7-12% of the patients felt that they could control the voices.

Several studies have attempted to assess the experienced or rated characteristics of voices in psychiatric patients, including perceived location, and relate them to clinical variables. Aggernaes (1972) found that AH were rated as highly similar to 'real' perceptions in every way except for 'publicness'; that is, only a third of his primarily chronic psychiatric patients felt that their voices could be heard by others. Oulis and colleagues (1995) carefully examined internal AH and found, in contrast to Jaspers (1963/1913), that they were experienced as 'real' as external AH[6]. Yee et al (2005) came to similar conclusions. However, in

TABLE 3. Perceived Location of AH in Psychiatric and Non-Patient Populations

Study	Sample	N	External	Internal	Both
Mott, Small & Anderson (1965)	schizophrenic medical	50 50	61% 76%[1]	33% 12% .	6% 12%
Judkins & Slade (1981)	schizophrenia[2]	26	31%	27%	42%
Junginger & Frame (1985)	mixed[3] psychiatric	52	46%	37%	17%[4]
Nayani & David (1996)	schizophrenic mixed[5] psychiatric	61 39	44% 56%	43% 31%	13% 13%
Honig et al (1998)	schizophrenic dissociative disorder non-patients[7]	18 15 15	50% 27% 40%	22% 33% 47%	28%[6] 40% 13%
Copolov, Trauer & Mackinnon (2004)	mixed[8] psychiatric	197	28%	34%	38%

[1] This percentage, the highest in this column, is due to the large presence of AH, almost 50%, involving the person's name being called distinctly enough to motivate a search for its source – clearly indicating the location of such AH as outside of the individual.

[2] Includes one diagnosis of psychotic depression.

[3] Diagnostic distribution (mixed inpatient and outpatient): 52% schizophrenic, 25% affective disorders, 23% other (including 7 – 13% – schizoaffective disorder).

[4] Histogram (Fig. 1) appears discrepant with reported sample size (*n*=52), as results for 54 subjects appear to be represented. Percentages calculated on *n*=54.

[5] Diagnostic distribution (mixed inpatient, outpatient, day treatment): 44% affective disorder, 18% schizoaffective, 18% paranoid psychosis, 9% alcohol hallucinosis, 11% other. Calculated from Table 1, which is discrepant with sample size listed in text (*n*=106 vs *n*=100).

[6] Honig et al (1998) did not utilize a 'both' category, including in both internal and external categories persons who heard both types of voices. Differences between groups are not significant.

[7] Recruited through media. No psychiatric history, evidence of current psychiatric disorder, or severe dissociative symptoms present.

[8] Diagnostic distribution (mixed inpatient and outpatient): 81% schizophrenic, 14% affective disorder, 5% other. No correlation between diagnosis and perceived location reported.

Oulis and colleagues' (1995) study, internal AH were rated as less hostile and were accompanied by significantly more insight than external AH.

A rich phenomenological study of AH in 100 psychiatric patients was conducted by Nayani and David (1996). As Nayani and David found more of the 'newer' psychiatric patients to experience external AH than the more 'experienced' patients, they inferred that AH might move from external to internal over time, with increasing voice engagement by the patient (consistent with Havens, 1962; Romme et al., 1992). This view was supported by their finding that internal AH were more grammatically and syntactically complex than external AH. Perceived location was unrelated to diagnosis, but internal AH were associated with increased insight.

In a recent cross-sectional study with a large sample ($n = 197$), Copolov and colleagues (2004) found few relationships between internal AH and other characteristics of the voices, other than increased insight. Diagnosis, positive or negative content, and level of medication usage were all unrelated to perceived AH location. Copolov and colleagues concluded that the perceived location of AH lacked clinical utility.

However, as none of the above studies screened for dissociative disorders, it may be premature to conclude that perceived location of voice(s) is ineffective in predicting diagnosis, only at differentiating between the various psychotic diagnoses included. Even so, the Honig and colleagues' (1998) study, which did carefully compare persons diagnosed schizophrenic with those with dissociative disorders, found no significant differences in this regard.

A number of authors have commented on voice hearers' relationships with their voices. Nayani and David (1996) found that multiple voice hearers had distinct relationships with their voices, and appeared to know intimate details of their life. Some consider such 'omniscience' to be an almost universal characteristic of voices (Chadwick & Birchwood, 1994). Nayani and David (1996) also found that the voices frequently spoke with different accents from those of the patients, but used ones which were always personally and/or culturally relevant to them. Others have noted strong linguistic and affective similarities to relationships found between persons in the 'real world' (Hoffman, Oates, Hafner, Hustig, & McGlashan, 1994). 1994; Miller, O'Connor, & Di Pasquale, 1993); the extended duration of AH episodes–30 minutes or more (Aggernaes, 1972; Oulis et al., 1995)–is also suggestive of this. Indeed, Benjamin (1989) reported that all patients in his study had "meaningful, integrated and interpersonally coherent relationships with their voices" (p. 309). Perhaps of most importance, Nayani and David (1996) found that patients who were unable (or unwilling?) to converse with their voices were considerably more distressed than patients who could dialogue with them.

Much of the above, including the findings of the perceived 'omniscience' of voices (Chadwick & Birchwood, 1994), are consistent with Jaynes' thesis that hearing voices is a normal part of human evolutionary history, and that contemporary AH derive directly from voices of 'gods' heard millennia ago. Jaynes believed that voices developed around the need to make novel decisions when human societies become more diversified and complex. His linking of AH with decision-making is echoed by Nayani and David (1996), who conclude that AH "bear a strong resemblance to patterns of thought that are part of the normal experience of making decisions" (p. 184). Such a view is also shared by Marius Romme and his colleagues in Maastricht, who attempt to determine early on, when working with a person who hears voices, what 'problem' the AH represents. Even Jaynes' speculation about the role of the right hemisphere in AH has received some support. Anthony David, after reviewing recent neuroimaging work, concluded that AH may involve "right auditory regions which are implicated in the processing of the prosodic aspects of speech" (David, 1999, p. 101). Clearly, Jaynes' theory, while not without its flaws, goes a long way toward explaining why AH remain so common today, and appear similar whether heard by psychiatric patients, grieving partners, traumatized children or tribal elders.

AH AND DISSOCIATIVE EXPERIENCES

While AH are clearly not unique to persons diagnosed with dissociative disorders, is it possible that dissociation is the mechanism underlying all forms of AH? It has long been acknowledged that dissociative symptoms are strongly related to traumatic experiences. Dissociative symptoms make up a core part of the diagnosis of Post-Traumatic Stress Disorder (PTSD) and particularly Acute Stress Disorder (APA, 1994). Traumatic or highly stressful experiences precede the development of AH in the vast majority of voice hearers (Heins, Gray, & Tennant, 1990; Romme & Escher, 1989) and childhood trauma appears more strongly related to AH than to other 'psychotic' symptoms (Ensink, 1992; Read & Argyle, 1999; Ross, Anderson, & Clark, 1994). While these studies link trauma with dissociation or with

AH, direct evidence relating psychotic symptoms in general, and AH in particular, to dissociative experiences has now been found.

Strong links between psychotic symptoms, including AH, and dissociative experiences in a wide range of clinical and non-patient populations have been demonstrated in a number of studies (reviewed in Moskowitz, Barker-Collo, & Ellson, 2004) and psychotic symptoms, particularly those considered pathognomic for DSM-IV schizophrenia, are commonly found in persons with DID (Kluft, 1987; Ross et al., 1990). Four studies have demonstrated robust links between AH and dissociative experiences. In a population of non-psychotic adolescents, primarily from a residential treatment center, Altman, Collins, and Mundy (1997) found that dissociative experiences, as measured by the Dissociative Experiences Scale (DES; Carlson & Putnam, 1986), strongly predicted AH, even after controlling for mood disturbance and schizotypal thought processes. Similarly, Kilcommons and Morrison (2005) found scores on the DES (particularly the *depersonalization* subscale) to significantly predict AH in psychotic patients (even after controlling for severity of trauma), and Morrison & Peterson (in press) found DES scores to correlate .71 with predisposition to AH in adult non-patients. Finally, Glicksohn and Barrett (2003), also looking at adult non-patients, found 25% shared variance between DES scores and measures of both AH and predisposition to AH. All of the above authors concluded that dissociation, in one form or another, was a 'predisposing factor' for AH.

PREDICTORS OF PSYCHOTIC SYMPTOMS AND MENTAL HEALTH SYSTEM CONTACT

If AH are indeed linked to dissociative experiences, as the evidence reported in the prior section indicates, what determines why some people, but not others, develop delusional explanations for these experiences and enter the mental health system? A longitudinal study in the Netherlands, following children and adolescents positive for hearing voices over a three-year period, has gone some way toward addressing this question. Sandra Escher, along with Marius Romme and their colleagues at the University of Maastricht, located 80 children and adolescents who acknowledged hearing voices when first contacted via media channels. Most of the participants no longer heard any voices by the end of the three-year period (Escher, Romme, Buiks, Delespaul, & Van Os, 2002a). Significant variables which distinguished children who continued to hear voices from those who did not, along with factors determining who developed delusions and received mental health system contact, were sought. Escher and colleagues found, consistent with Morrison's (1998) model of voice persistence, that clinician-rated anxiety and depression were the strongest predictors of voice continuation; they were also the best predictor of who developed delusions and received professional mental health care (Escher et al., 2002a; Escher, Romme, Buiks, Delespaul, & Van Os, J, 2002b; Escher, Morris, Buiks, Delespaul, Van Os, & Romme, 2004). Other factors predicting voice persistence included clinician-rated severity and frequency of AH at baseline, dissociation scores (children who continued to hear voices reported more dissociative experiences than children whose voices stopped), and lack of clear spatial and temporal triggers (Escher et al., 2002a). Significantly, neither mental health contact nor the development of delusions was related to voice continuation.

With regard to mental health system contact, Escher and colleagues found the voices of children who received care to be rated as more severe, and having more impact on their emotions and actions, than children who did not enter the mental health system. Not surprisingly, this group also reported more 'problem behavior' than children who did not receive care (Escher et al., 2004). In addition, delusions were associated more strongly with external than internal voices in the older children (i.e., 13 years or above) but not in the younger ones (Escher et al., 2002b). Dissociation scores were unrelated to the development of delusions in this population (Escher et al., 2002b). As noted above, they were also unrelated to mental health system contact, but did predict voice persistence (Escher et al., 2002a, 2004).

Finally, if AH appearing in persons designated psychotic do not, in fact, appear different from AH appearing in other persons, can they be treated similarly?

CLINICAL APPROACHES TO AH

It is becoming increasingly acknowledged that AH do not typically respond directly to psychiatric medications; if they are effective, it is argued that this occurs through decreasing the distress experienced by the voice hearer (Kapur, 2003). This has also become the approach advocated for psychotherapeutic methods of dealing with AH (Chadwick, Birchwood, & Trower, 1996; Kingdon & Turkington, 2005). Such approaches do not attempt to address AH directly, but rather to deal with the responses to and assumptions about AH.

However, some clinicians, such as Colin Ross (2004), are proposing that AH be dealt with in a manner similar to that long considered standard in the field of dissociative disorders. As typical treatment of DID often involves direct therapeutic engagement with many if not all of the personality parts or alters (Putnam, 1989), might it not be possible for a therapist to directly engage with the AH heard by the voice hearer? This proposal is not as radical as it might sound, as having the person directly communicate with his or her voices in the presence of the therapist is now being advocated in cases of PTSD in which AH are experienced (Brewin, 2003).

The second author of this article, working closely with Marius Romme and Sandra Escher, has extensive experience in engaging with voices in the manner described above. Over the past 10 years, several dozen voice hearers in the vicinity of Maastricht in the Netherlands have allowed their voices to be directly worked with, in a variant of the Voice Dialogue approach (Stone and Winkelman, 1989). In this approach, the therapist asks permission from the voice hearer to directly speak with his or her voices, and then proceeds to–quite respectfully–'interview' the voice as one might a new acquaintance. The timing and reasons for the voice coming into being, its relation to the person, and what it 'wants' are all explored. This is repeated for all voices (that allow contact), with the person usually taking a different chair in the room for each voice. The Maastricht approach also includes other psychosocial interventions.

Typical results can include a decrease in the perceived 'destructiveness' of the voices, including a transformation from 'negative' to 'positive' voices with increased understanding from the person, along with an increased capacity (and willingness) to dialogue with the voices. No person has so far become more psychotic, and quality of life is sometimes substantially improved. A key variable in the effectiveness of this treatment appears to be whether or not the person can (or believes they can) dialogue with their voices. If they cannot, then the therapist also cannot work with the voices. The following clinical vignette illustrates this approach to working with AH.

CASE ILLUSTRATION

'Karen' presented for treatment shortly after leaving a psychiatric hospital where she had been living for the prior four years, struggling with hostile and command AH and suicidal ideation. During her contact with the mental health system, she had been diagnosed (at various times) as suffering from schizophrenia or borderline personality disorder, and received antipsychotic and other medications which helped reduce her feelings of anxiety and fear but did not directly impact on the voices. Karen had heard voices (from outside her head) since she was a child, but functioned well–working as a secretary–until around 20 years old when she joined a religious sect. When the sect members were informed about Karen's voices, she was told that they were 'instruments of the devil' and instructed to get rid of them. From that point on, the four male voices became more negative and disturbing, commenting on Karen's behavior and her thinking and telling her to kill herself[7]. The only ways she had of coping with them were to ignore them, go to sleep, isolate herself or argue with them when she could no longer bear it. None of these strategies worked particularly well.

At the first session, the therapist asked Karen for permission to talk to the voices. She agreed and each voice was interviewed in turn. They all told the same story. They reported that they came into Karen's life when she was about four, when she was feeling quite lonely (and around the time, it later emerged, that she had been sexually abused), and served as her companions. Their job was to help Karen feel less lonely and overcome difficult moments. Before she joined the sect, Karen accepted the voices and they felt acknowledged. However, afterwards everything changed. As Karen's attitude to the voices changed, as she began to reject them, so they too rejected her–becoming very negative and telling her to kill herself. Her initial admission to the hospital was precipitated by her finally giving in to the voices and attempting to kill herself.

In speaking with the therapist, the voices requested that Karen again accept them, as she had in the beginning. Karen, who was able to 'overhear' the therapist talking with the voices, agreed and began setting aside time in the evening to engage with the voices. By the next session, two of the voices had disappeared, and those that remained were easy to ignore. The voices became more positive, no longer criticizing Karen or exhorting her to kill herself. After a few more, largely supportive, sessions the therapy was completed. When she contacted the therapist four years later, she reported that she was happy (despite being divorced) and was living with her two young children in a new city. She had not been psychiatrically hospitalized since the treatment, and remained on a very low dose of antipsychotic medication. Karen now heard only one voice, but it was one she liked to talk to it because it was positive and supportive.

DISCUSSION:
AH AS NON-PATHOLOGICAL
DISSOCIATIVE EXPERIENCES

On balance, the above historical, clinical, and research evidence does not suggest that AH appearing in psychotic disorders can, on the basis of their experienced characteristics, be distinguished from AH reported by persons with no mental health system contact. Instead, a diagnosis of schizophrenia or another psychotic disorder and psychiatric treatment in persons with AH appears to be most strongly related to the level of depression and anxiety those voices foster (Close & Garety, 1998; Escher et al., 2002a, 2002b, 2004; Morrison, 1998). Persons who are able to cope well with the voices, particularly those that are able to engage the voices and reach "some sort of peaceful accommodation and acceptance of the voice as 'part of me'" (Romme & Escher, 1989, p. 44), either do not enter the mental health system at all or exit the system successfully (Nayani & David, 1996). In this way, AH can be conceptualized as behaving similarly to a trauma (an argument that has previously been made (e.g., Frame & Morrison, 2001; Meyer, Taiminen, Vuori, Aijala, & Helenius, 1999) in that it is the person's response to the trauma or AH, and in particular the extent to which they can incorporate it into their existing schemas (or successfully modify them) that determines whether they will draw the attention of a mental health professional[8].

While others have previously argued that AH should be considered essentially 'normal' phenomena (Morrison, 1998; Romme & Escher, 1989), no one, as far as we are aware, has taken this position to its logical conclusion: that AH should no longer be considered psychotic symptoms, but simply one of a number of experiences (including various traumas) that can, under certain circumstances, induce delusions and lead to entry into the mental health system. Further, we believe that the evidence is strong enough to argue that, not only are voices non-pathological phenomena, but that they are dissociative in nature. As such, our position goes further than that of authors who have argued that dissociative experiences provide a predisposition or diathesis for AH (Allen & Coyne, 1995; Glicksohn, 2004); it is closer to the positions of Merckelbach et al. (2000) and Watson (2001), who question whether the concepts of dissociation and psychosis are, in fact, distinguishable.

It is almost axiomatic at this point to assert that AH result from the 'misattribution' of internal experiences to external sources (Bentall, 1990; Morrison, 1998). Various cognitive mechanisms have been posited to explain such mistakes (drive to maintain self-esteem (Bentall, 1990); cognitive dissonance (Morrison, 1998)), but such explanations seem unsatisfactory. Perhaps they can explain why some thoughts are experienced as 'intrusive' or 'inserted' (i.e., not belonging to me), but they are less successful in explaining how such extruded thoughts become 'heard.' Further, we would argue that dissociative mechanisms are needed to explain the central experience of AH–that of an 'other' relating to one's 'self.' It is hard to see how one can have a relationship with an extruded or projected thought; engaging in a relationship is consistently how the experience of AH is described.

However, conceiving of AH as dissociative phenomena does not solve the enigma of voices. Several questions about diagnostic and clinical utility remain, calling for future research:

1. Is perceived location completely irrelevant? Despite all of the research reported in this paper, more thorough investigation needs to be done before this question can be put to rest. Do AH really move from external to internal with successful coping or treatment, as several have suggested (Havens, 1962; Nayani & David, 1996; Romme et al., 1992)? What about voice hearers who have both internal and external voices? Are the external voices more ego-dystonic than the internal ones?

2. Is the public/private dimension more important than the internal/external dimension? While these dimensions often overlap, they are not the same. A confusion (or diffusion) between public and private worlds seems to bespeak a high level of pathology. Most people who hear voices, internal or external, do not believe they can be heard by others (Aggernaes, 1972; indeed, for many years, the standard clinical inquiry about AH was, "Do you hear voices other people can't hear?"), and some people believe that their thoughts are projected and can be picked up by others. Perhaps significantly, this symptom of 'thought projection' or 'thought broadcasting' (a delusion by definition) is very rare in dissociative disorders and borderline personality disorder, in contrast to other Schneiderian symptoms such as thought insertion and thought withdrawal (which can simply be accurate descriptions of unusual internal experiences; Kluft, 1987; Ross et al., 1990; Yee et al., 2005), but is quite common in persons diagnosed with schizophrenia (Peralta & Cuesta, 1999; Tandon & Greden, 1987). This suggests that the public/private dimension might have diagnostic implications, and could be a more fruitful area to explore than the internal/external dimension.

3. What determines why some people can engage with their voices and others cannot–a factor seemingly so important to their recovery? Is it that persons cannot engage or simply are afraid to? Typically, benevolent seeming voices are engaged with and 'malevolent' voices resisted (Chadwick & Birchwood, 1994;

Close & Garety, 1998), but this doesn't seem to be the whole picture. As seen in the clinical vignette, voices that are initially benevolent can turn malevolent when they are ignored. Further, it may be that the ability to engage with voices is a skill, related perhaps to dissociative capacities. Recall that Escher and colleagues (2002a) found that dissociation correlated with voice persistence, but was unrelated to psychotic diagnosis or mental health treatment. Is it necessary to 'cultivate' the voice, to nurture it in a sense, in order to engage with it? Here is what Mark Vonnegut (probably highly dissociative as he experienced amnesic episodes, uncommon in schizophrenia; Steinberg, 1995) had to say about his initial AH experiences:

At first I'd had to strain to hear or understand them. They were soft and working with some pretty tricky codes. Snap-crackle-pops, the sound of the wind with blinking lights and horns for punctuation. I broke the code and somehow was able to internalize it to the point where it was just like hearing words. (Vonnegut, 1975, p. 106)

Over time, his AH experiences was transformed.

The voices weren't much fun in the beginning. Part of it was simply my being uncomfortable about hearing voices no matter what they had to say, but the early voices were mostly bearers of bad news. Besides, they didn't seem to like me much and there was no way I could talk back to them . . . But later the voices could be very pleasant. They'd often be the voice of someone I loved, and even if they weren't, I could talk too, asking questions about this or that and getting reasonable answers. They were very important messages that had to get through somehow. More orthodox channels like phone and mail had broken down. (Vonnegut, 1975, p. 106)

Finally, where does de-coupling the concept of AH from psychosis leave the latter concept? We would suggest - in tatters. The DSM-IV does not have an adequate diagnosis of psychosis; all it does is refer back to symptoms considered psychotic. Indeed, it offers three different definitions, progressively broader: (1) delusions and prominent hallucinations experienced without insight, (2) delusions and prominent hallucinations (regardless of insight), and (3) the four Criterion A positive symptoms of schizophrenia (i.e., delusions, hallucinations, disorganized speech, and grossly disorganized behavior or catatonic behavior).

The arguments for considering disorganized speech and disorganized/catatonic behavior are weak and have been discussed elsewhere (Moskowitz et al., submitted). Briefly, either symptom may be due to speech or behavior that is relevant to a context of which the listener/observer is unaware (and as such, is *not* disorganized); one only has to consider the speech and behavior of a person experiencing a trauma flashback, and imagine how their behavior would be interpreted if the observer was unaware of their history, to see this.

Thus, we are left with only delusions as the paradigmatic psychotic symptom. As such, it is difficult to see what the concept of psychosis adds to the concept of delusions. Perhaps this concept should simply be dispensed with, and persons experiencing delusions should be referred to simply as–delusional. The questionable validity of the concept of psychosis has obvious implications for the validity of the current concept of schizophrenia, as the two concepts are closely wedded in the DSM-IV. That, however, is beyond the purview of this article.

In conclusion, the evidence supports our view that AH: (a) are best conceptualized as dissociative experiences which appear in individuals predisposed, for reasons not yet clear, to hear voices when under stress, (b) require 'cultivation' or 'nurturing' to make their meaning clear, (c) resolve when appropriately engaged with by the individual, possibly moving from externally- to internally-perceived in the process, and (d) are consistent with Jaynes' evolutionary theory of the bicameral mind. Accordingly, we call on our mental health colleagues to no longer designate AH as a psychotic symptom, to conduct research on the remaining areas of confusion in AH (such as determining those factors influencing engagement with voices), and to explore alternative ways of working with the voices heard by many of us.

NOTES

1. Technically, the term auditory hallucinations refers to any sound heard in the absence of appropriate external stimuli, not only voices. For example, during post-traumatic flashbacks, a wide range of sounds related to a trauma, such as police sirens, gunshots, etc., may be heard. However, for the purposes of this article, auditory hallucinations will be used exclusively to refer to the hearing of voices. While voices are sometimes referred to as 'verbal' hallucinations, the term auditory hallucinations is more familiar and as such is preferred here.

2. We do not take a position in this paper as to whether AH may, under some circumstances, represent a 'genuine' spiritual experience. Even if that is allowed, however, adequate means to distinguish such experiences from AH better explained by psychological (dissociative) mechanisms remains to be established. In other words, at least some AH interpreted by the voice hearer as spiritual may actually derive from a

disowned aspect of themselves. At this point, we cannot adequately distinguish between the two on the basis of reported experience.

3. The term 'pseudo-hallucination' was coined in 1868 by Hagen to refer to hallucinations with less sensory 'fullness' than perceptions (or 'true' hallucinations), which derived from an 'organ of apperception', and which were due to the spontaneous activity of memory (Berrios & Denning, 1996). Almost all theorists have considered 'pseudo-hallucinations' to be essentially normal phenomena.

4. Examples given of bizarre delusions are beliefs of loss of control of mind or body, and include delusions of control, and delusions of thought insertion and thought withdrawal (APA, 1994). Both of these sets of delusions, along with voices commenting and conversing, also delimit three of the four pathognomic symptoms of ICD-10 Schizophrenia (WHO, 1993). Some question whether these should be called delusions at all, as opposed to adequate descriptions of unusual/anomalous experiences (Spitzer, 1990). All are common in DID, where they are typically understood as deriving from the influence of one part of the personality on another (Kluft, 1987; Ross et al., 1989; Ross et al., 1990).

5. A seventh, Wiles et al (2006), is not reported here because incidence and not prevalence data were used. Of interest, however, is that just over 5% of almost 2000 persons, without a psychiatric history and not meeting criteria for a psychotic disorder, reported at least one of four narrowly defined psychotic symptoms (thought insertion, paranoia, 'strange experiences' and hallucinations; Wiles et al., 2006).

6. Oulis et al (1995) reported that patients had little difficulty in identifying the location from which their voice(s) appeared to emanate, a finding confirmed by most other researchers.

7. As Karen also heard two or more voices conversing with each other, her voices fulfilled *both* of the pathognomic AH criteria for DSM-IV schizophrenia (i.e., voices commenting and voices conversing).

8. Indeed, Morrison's (1998) model of how 'normal' AH lead to psychopathology, in which he argues that AH may be 'misinterpreted' as "threatening the physical or psychological integrity of the individual," leading to decreased mood, hyperarousal and hypervigilance, along with avoidance behaviors (p. 296), almost exactly mirrors current conceptions of PTSD.

REFERENCES

Aggernaes, A. (1972). The experienced reality of hallucinations and other psychological phenomena. *Acta Psychiatrica Scandinavica, 45*, 220-238.

Allen, J. G., & Coyne, L. (1995). Dissociation and vulnerability to psychotic experience: The Dissociative Experiences Scale and the MMPI-2. *Journal of Nervous & Mental Disease, 183*, 615-622.

Altman, H., Collins, M., & Mundy, P. (1997). Subclinical hallucinations and delusions in nonpsychotic adolescents. *Journal of Child Psychology & Psychiatry & Allied Disciplines, 38*, 413-420.

American Psychiatric Association. (1994). *Diagnostic and statistical manual of mental disorders* (4th ed.). Washington, DC: American Psychiatric Association.

Barrett, T. R., & Etheridge, J. B. (1992). Verbal hallucinations in normals. I. People who hear voices. *Applied Cognitive Psychology, 6*, 379-387.

Benjamin, L. (1989). Is chronicity a function of the relationship between the person and the auditory hallucination? *Schizophrenia Bulletin, 15*, 291-310.

Bentall, R. P. (1990). The illusion of reality: a review and integration of psychological research on hallucinations. *Psychological Bulletin, 107*, 82-95.

Berrios, G. E., & Dening, T. R. (1996). Pseudohallucinations: A conceptual history. *Psychological Medicine, 26*, 753-763.

Brewin, C. R. (2003). *Posttraumatic stress disorder: Malady or myth.* New Haven, Connecticut: Yale University Press.

Carlson, E. B., & Putnam, F. W. (1986). Development, reliability, and validity of a dissociation scale. *Journal of Nervous & Mental Disease, 174*, 727-733.

Chadwick, P., & Birchwood, M. (1994). The omnipotence of voices: A cognitive approach to auditory hallucinations. *British Journal of Psychiatry, 164*, 190-201.

Chadwick, P., Birchwood, M., & Trower, P. (1996). *Cognitive therapy for delusions, voices, and paranoia.* Chichester, U.K.: John Wiley and Sons.

Close, H., & Garety, P. (1998). Cognitive assessment of voices: Further developments in understanding the emotional impact of voices. *British Journal of Clinical Psychology, 37*, 173-188.

Copolov, D. L., Trauer, T., & Mackinnon, A. (2004). On the non-significance of internal versus external auditory hallucinations. *Schizophrenia Research, 69*, 1-6.

David, A. S. (1999). Auditory hallucinations: phenomenology, neuropsychology and neuroimaging update. *Acta Psychiatrica Scandinavica, 99*, 95-104.

Dening, T. R., & Berrios, G. E. (1996). The enigma of pseudohallucinations: Current meanings and usage. *Psychopathology, 29*, 27-34.

Derogatis, L. R. (1994). *Symptom Checklist-90-R (SCL-90-R) administration, scoring, and procedures manual* (3rd ed.). Minneapolis: National Computer Systems.

Dhossche, D., Ferdinand, R., Van der Ende, J., Hofstra, M. B., & Verhulst, F. (2002). Diagnostic outcome of self-reported hallucinations in a community sample of adolescents. *Psychological Medicine, 32*, 619-627.

Ensink, B. J. (1992). *Confusing realities: A study on child sexual abuse and psychiatric symptoms.* Amsterdam: VU Press.

Escher, S., Romme, M., Buiks, A., Delespaul, P., & Van Os, J. (2002a). Independent course of childhood auditory hallucinations: A sequential 3-year follow up study. *British Journal of Psychiatry, 181 (suppl. 43)*, s10-s18.

Escher, S., Romme, M., Buiks, A., Delespaul, P., & van Os, J. (2002b). Formation of delusional ideation in adolescents hearing voices: A prospective study. *American Journal of Medical Genetics, 114*, 913-920.

Escher, A., Morris, M., Buiks, A., Delespaul, P., Van Os, J., & Romme, M. (2004). Determinants of outcome in the pathways through care for children hearing voices. *International Journal of Social Welfare, 13*, 208-222.

Frame, L., & Morrison, A. P. (2001). Causes of posttraumatic stress disorder in psychotic patients. *Archives of General Psychiatry, 58*, 305-306.

Glicksohn, J. (2004). Absorption, hallucinations, and the continuum hypothesis. *Behavioral & Brain Sciences, 27*, 793-794.

Glicksohn, J., & Barrett, T. R. (2003). Absorption and hallucinatory experience. *Applied Cognitive Psychology, 17*(7), 833-849.

Hare, E. H. (1973). A short note on pseudo-hallucinations. *British Journal of Psychiatry, 122*, 469-476.

Hathaway, S., & McKinley, J. (1967). *Minnesota Multiphasic Personality Inventory manual revised*. New York: The Psychological Corporation.

Havens, L. (1962). The placement and movement of hallucinations in space: Phenomenology and theory. *International Journal of Psychoanalysis, 43,* 426-435.

Heins, T., Gray, A., & Tennant, M. (1990). Persisting hallucinations following childhood sexual abuse. *Australian & New Zealand Journal of Psychiatry, 24,* 561-565.

Hoffman, R. E., Oates, E., Hafner, J., Hustig, H. H., & McGlashan, T. H. (1994). Semantic organization of hallucinated 'voices' in schizophrenia. *American Journal of Psychiatry, 151,* 1229-1230.

Honig, A., Romme, M. A. J., Ensink, B. J., Escher, S. D. M. A. C., Pennings, M. H. A., & deVries, M. W. (1998). Auditory hallucinations: A comparison between patients and nonpatients. *Journal of Nervous & Mental Disease, 186,* 646-651.

Jaspers, K. (1963). *General Psychopathology* (J. Hoenig & M. W. Hamilton, Trans.). Manchester, UK: Manchester University Press. (Original publication date 1913).

Jaynes, J. (1976). *The Origin of Consciousness in the Breakdown of the Bicameral Mind*. Boston: Houghton Mifflin.

Johns, L. C., Nazroo, J. Y., Bebbington, P., & Kuipers, E. (2002). Occurrence of hallucinatory experiences in a community sample and ethnic variations. *British Journal of Psychiatry, 180,* 174-178.

Kapur, S. (2003). Psychosis as a state of aberrant salience: A framework linking biology, phenomenology, and pharmacology in schizophrenia. *American Journal of Psychiatry, 160,* 13-23.

Kilcommons, A. M., & Morrison, A. P. (2005). Relationships between trauma and psychosis: an exploration of cognitive and dissociative factors. *Acta Psychiatrica Scandinavica, 112,* 351-359.

Kingdon, D. G., & Turkington, D. (2005). *Cognitive therapy of schizophrenia*. New York: Guilford Press.

Kluft, R. P. (1987). First-rank symptoms as a diagnostic clue to multiple personality disorder. *American Journal of Psychiatry, 144,* 293-298.

Merckelbach, H., Rassin, E., & Muris, P. (2000). Dissociation, schizotypy, and fantasy proneness in undergraduate students. *Journal of Nervous and Mental Disease, 188,* 428-431.

Meyer, H., Taiminen, T., Vuori, T., Aijala, A., & Helenius, H. (1999). Posttraumatic stress disorder symptoms related to psychosis and acute involuntary hospitalization in schizophrenic and delusional patients. *Journal of Nervous and Mental Disease, 187,* 343-352.

Miller, L. J., O'Connor, E., & Di Pasquale, T. (1993). Patients' attitudes toward hallucinations. *American Journal of Psychiatry, 150,* 584-588.

Morrison, A. P. (1998). A cognitive analysis of the maintenance of auditory hallucinations: Are voices to schizophrenia what bodily sensations are to panic? *Behavioural and Cognitive Psychotherapy, 26,* 289-302.

Morrison, A. P., & Peterson, T. (in press). Trauma, metacognition and predisposition to hallucinations in non-patients. *Behavioral and Cognitive Psychotherapy*.

Moskowitz, A., Barker-Collo, S., & Ellson, L. (2004). Replication of dissociation-psychoticism link in New Zealand students and inmates. *Journal of Nervous and Mental Disease, 193,* 722-727.

Moskowitz, A. K., Read, J., Farrelly, S., Rudegeair, T., & Williams, O. (2007). Are psychotic symptoms traumatic in origin and dissociative in kind? In P. F. Dell & J. O'Neil (Eds.), *Dissociation and the Dissociative Disorders: DSM-V and Beyond.* Routledge: New York.

Mott, R. H., Small, I. F., & Anderson, J. M. (1965). A comparative study of hallucinations. *Archives of General Psychiatry, 12,* 595-601.

Nayani, T. H., & David, A. S. (1996). The auditory hallucination: a phenomenological survey. *Psychological Medicine, 26,* 177-189.

Nurcombe, B., Mitchell, W., Begtrup, R., Tramontana, M., LaBarbera, J., & Pruitt, J. (1996). Dissociative hallucinosis and allied conditions. In F. R. Volkmar (Ed.), *Psychoses and pervasive developmental disorders in childhood and adolescence.* Washington, DC: American Psychiatric Press.

Ohayon, M. M. (2000). Prevalence of hallucinations and their pathological associations in the general population. *Psychiatry Research, 97,* 153-164.

Oulis, P. G., Mavreas, V. G., Mamounas, J. M., & Stefanis, C. N. (1995). Clinical characteristics of auditory hallucinations. *Acta Psychiatrica Scandinavica, 92,* 97-102.

Peralta, V., & Cuesta, M. J. (1999). Diagnostic significance of Schneider's first-rank symptoms in schizophrenia. *British Journal of Psychiatry, 174,* 243-248.

Posey, T. B., & Losch, M. E. (1983). Auditory hallucinations of hearing voices in 375 normal subjects. *Imagination, Cognition and Personality, 3,* 99-113.

Putnam, F. W. (1989). *Diagnosis and treatment of Multiple Personality Disorder.* New York: Guilford Press.

Read, J., & Argyle, N. (1999). Hallucinations, delusions, and thought disorder Among adult psychiatric inpatients with a history of child abuse. *Psychiatric Services, 50,* 1467-1472.

Romme, M. A. J., & Escher, D. M. A. C. (1989). Hearing voices. *Schizophrenia Bulletin, 15,* 40-47.

Romme, M. A. J., Honig, A., Noorthoorn, E. O., & Escher, A. D. M. A. C. (1992). Coping with hearing voices: An emancipatory approach. *British Journal of Psychiatry, 161,* 99-103.

Ross, C. A. (2004). *Schizophrenia: Innovations in diagnosis and treatment.* New York: The Haworth Press, Inc.

Ross, C. A., Anderson, G., & Clark, P. (1994). Childhood abuse and the positive symptoms of schizophrenia. *Hospital & Community Psychiatry, 45,* 489-491.

Ross, C. A., Heber, S., Norton, G. R., & Anderson, G. (1989). Differences between multiple personality disorder and other diagnostic groups on structured interview. *Journal of Nervous and Mental Disease, 177,* 487-491.

Ross, C. A., Miller, S. D., Reagor, P., Bjornson, L., Fraser, G. A., & Anderson, G. (1990). Schneiderian symptoms in multiple personality disorder and schizophrenia. *Comprehensive Psychiatry, 31,* 111-118.

Sarbin, T. R., & Juhasz, J. B. (1967). The historical background of the concept of hallucination. *Journal of the History of the Behavioral Sciences, 5,* 339-358.

Sedman, G. (1966a). A comparative study of pseudohallucinations, imagery and true hallucinations. *British Journal of Psychiatry, 112,* 9-17.

Sedman, G. (1966b). "Inner voices." Phenomenological and clinical aspects. *British Journal of Psychiatry, 112,* 485-490.

Sedman, G. (1966c). A phenomenological study of pseudohallucinations and related experiences. *Acta Psychiatrica Scandinavica, 42*, 35-70.

Schneider, K. (1959). *Clinical Psychopathology* (5th ed.). New York: Grune and Stratton.

Sidgewick, H., Johnson, A., Myers, F. W. H., et al. (1894). Report on the census of hallucinations. *Proceedings of the Society for Psychical Research, 26*, 259-394.

Spitzer, M. (1990). On defining delusions. *Comprehensive Psychiatry, 31*, 377-397.

Steinberg, M. (1995). *Handbook for the assessment of dissociation: A clinical guide.* Washington, DC: American Psychiatric Press.

Stone, H., & Winkelman, S. (1989). *Embracing our selves: The Voice Dialogue manual.* Novato, California: Nataraj Publishing.

Tandon, R., & Greden, J. F. (1987). Schneiderian first rank symptoms: Reconfirmation of high specificity for schizophrenia. *Acta Psychiatrica Scandinavica, 75*, 392-396.

Taylor, F. K. (1981). On pseudo-hallucinations. *Psychological Medicine, 11*, 265-271.

Tien, A. Y. (1991). Distributions of hallucinations in the population. *Social Psychiatry and Psychiatric Epidemiology, 26*, 287-292.

Van der Zwaard, R., & Polak, M. A. (2001). Pseudohallucinations: a pseudoconcept? A review of the validity of the concept, related to associate symptomatology. *Comprehensive Psychiatry, 42*, 42-50.

Van Os, J., Hanssen, M., Bijl, R. V., & Ravelli, A. (2000). Strauss (1969) revisited: A psychosis continuum in the general population? *Schizophrenia Research, 45*, 11-20.

Vonnegut, M. (1975). *The Eden Express.* New York: Praeger.

Yee, L., Korner, A. K., McSwiggan, S., Meares, R. A., & Stevenson, J. (2005). Persistant hallucinosis in borderline personality disorder. *Comprehensive Psychiatry, 46*, 147-154.

Watson, D. (2001). Dissociations of the night: Individual differences in sleep-related experiences and their relation to dissociation and schizotypy. *Journal of Abnormal Psychology, 110*, 526-535.

Wiles, N., Sammit, S., Bebbington, P., Singleton, N., Meltzer, H., & Lewis, G. (2006). Self-reported psychotic symptoms in the general population. *British Journal of Psychiatry, 188*, 519-526.

doi:10.1300/J513v06n02_04

EMPIRICAL STUDIES

Impact of Child Abuse Timing
and Family Environment on Psychosis

Jan Faust
Lindsay M. Stewart

SUMMARY. The theoretical basis for the development of differential psychopathology in children in response to a traumatic event suggests the timing of trauma and the family environment likely influence the development of psychological disturbances. We predicted that abused children who had psychotic symptoms would have experienced the trauma earlier in life than those children diagnosed with post traumatic stress disorder (PTSD). We also predicted that children with psychotic symptoms would hail from homes higher in cohesion and family conflict than those children with PTSD. Participants were 40 children, ages 6 to 17, and their mothers. All children were receiving treatment at a community mental health center, and were diagnosed with either posttraumatic stress disorder (PTSD; $n = 20$) or a psychotic based disorder ($n = 20$). Results indi-

Jan Faust and Lindsay M. Stewart are both affiliated with Nova Southeastern University.

This research was supported in part by an NIMH grant (# 1R29MH50340-01A3) awarded to the first author.

[Haworth co-indexing entry note]: "Impact of Child Abuse Timing and Family Environment on Psychosis." Faust, Jan, and Lindsay M. Stewart. Co-published simultaneously in *Journal of Psychological Trauma* (The Haworth Maltreatment & Trauma Press, an imprint of The Haworth Press) Vol. 6, No. 2/3, 2007, pp. 65-85; and: *Trauma and Serious Mental Illness* (ed: Steven N. Gold, and Jon D. Elhai) The Haworth Maltreatment & Trauma Press, an imprint of The Haworth Press, 2007, pp. 65-85. Single or multiple copies of this article are available for a fee from The Haworth Document Delivery Service [1-800-HAWORTH, 9:00 a.m. - 5:00 p.m. (EST). E-mail address: docdelivery@haworthpress.com].

cated that children with psychotic disorders experienced trauma earlier than children with PTSD *(p < .02)*. Children with psychotic disorders reported more familial conflict *(p < .04)* than those children with PTSD. When compared to mothers of children with PTSD, mothers of psychotic children rated their family as less cohesive *(p < .03)*. Implications of this research were discussed. doi:10.1300/J513v06n02_05 *[Article copies available for a fee from The Haworth Document Delivery Service: 1-800-HAWORTH. E-mail address: <docdelivery@haworthpress.com> Website: <http://www.HaworthPress.com> © 2007 by The Haworth Press, Inc. All rights reserved.]*

KEYWORDS. Child abuse, PTSD, psychosis

Over the years scientists have implicated both environmental and biological factors as responsible for the onset of psychosis (Asarnow, Asarnow, Hornstein, & Russell, 1991; Volkmar, 1996). While both biological and psychosocial factors have been postulated throughout the history of psychology as contributing to the development of schizophrenia (cf., Bateson, Jackson, Haley, & Weakland, 1956; Freud, 1911; Fromm-Reichman, 1948; Kaplan, Sadock, & Grebb, 1994, Asarnow et al., 1991; Volkmar, 1996), it is unclear as to whether the biological influences are causally connected to schizophrenia and other psychotic disorders or are the result of having the disorder. Additionally it has also been proffered that many secondary symptoms of schizophrenia are the result of long term medication use (Karon & Vandenbos, 1994).

One of the most noxious psychosocial stressors an individual can encounter is exposure to interpersonal trauma such as child abuse. Concomitantly, one of the most common reactions to child maltreatment that has been observed scientifically is post traumatic stress disorder (PTSD); additionally, there is an emerging body of literature that indicates that those individuals who develop a thought disorder may in fact have been exposed to severe forms of interpersonal trauma in childhood. For example, Goldberg and Garno (2005) noted histories of severe child abuse in their sample diagnosed with bipolar disorder. Lysaker, Beattie, Strasburger, and Davis (2005) and Schenkel, Spaulding, DiLillo, and Silverstein (2005) observed the severity of symptoms in their schizophrenic populations was related to a child abuse history.

TRAUMA: PTSD AND PSYCHOTIC DISORDERS

Trauma and PTSD

The trauma literature is replete with studies indicating that child sexual abuse has an immediate as well as a long term impact on children to the extent that the deleterious effects of such abuse on children can be observed in adulthood (e.g., Browne & Finkelhor, 1986; Goldberg & Garno, 2005; Meston, Rellini, & Heiman, 2006; Stovall-McClough & Cloitre, 2006; Tharringer, Krivacska, Laye-McDonough, & Jamison, 1988). One of the most common psychological sequelae of child trauma exposure such as abuse is Post Traumatic Stress Disorder (PTSD). Although child victimization and PTSD research have lagged behind that of adults, there is increasing evidence that PTSD can be readily detected in child abuse populations. As early as 1988, McLeer, Deblinger, Atkins, and Foa reported that nearly half of their sexually abused child sample met DSM III-R criteria for PTSD, a finding supported by the work of others (Deblinger, McLeer, Atkins, Ralphe, & Foa, 1989; Faust, Furdella, & Villa, 2004; Wolfe, Gentile, & Wolfe, 1989). Additionally, Tremblay, Hebert, and Piche (2000) observed more anxiety, depressive, and dissociative symptoms in a sexually abused group of children meeting criteria for Type II traumatic stress than in their control groups. Parents of sexually abused children also reported that their children experienced more dissociative symptoms than the other groups. The sexually abused group manifested more aggressive behaviors and used avoidant coping strategies more frequently than the two comparison groups. Also, Hall (1999) discovered that those children who were diagnosed as meeting full criteria for PTSD and who experienced the greatest amount of negative events scored the highest on an assessment of complex trauma symptoms.

Other traumas such as natural disasters (e.g., hurricane) and man-made disasters (e.g., terrorism) have been implicated as precipitants in childhood onset of PTSD. For example, researchers discovered trauma symptoms in children exposed to the Oklahoma City bombing (Pfefferbaum et al., 1999) and others observed post trauma symptoms in children exposed to hurricanes (LaGreca, Silverman, Vernberg, & Prinstein, 1996; LaGreca, Silverman, Vernberg, & Roberts, 2002).

Trauma and Psychosis

Research on trauma and mental illness has traditionally focused on the relationship between traumatic experiences (e.g., child abuse) and non-psychotic disorders, such as PTSD. In contrast, the possibility of such a relationship for psychotic disorders is often dismissed (Read, Van Os, & Morrison, 2005). This latter phenomenon may reflect the commonly held presumption, the more severe the mental illness, the more likely it is to have a genetic or biological basis. However, there is now evidence to suggest that the trauma of child sexual and physical abuse is linked to both PTSD and psychosis.

Historical and current psychosocial stressors that have been identi-fied as a contributory cause of schizophrenia and other psychotic disor-ders include toxic family interactions (Kavanagh, 1992), children's perception of the family environment as dysfunctional (Bateson, Jack-son, & Weakland, 1963), as well as incidences of interpersonal trauma (Livingston, 1987). It is likely that psychosocial stressors such as fam-ily-related variables interact to contribute to the onset of psychosis. Fur-thermore, because the nature of these interactions may be different at different points in development, traumatic stressors experienced in early childhood may lead to more serious mental health outcomes than trauma experienced later in development.

Although only a handful of studies have explored the relationship be-tween sexual and physical abuse and psychosis in children, the fre-quency of child abuse episodes reported by adult patients with psychotic disorders strongly supports the existence of such a relation-ship. Livingston (1987) found that 77% of child inpatients who had been sexually abused were diagnosed as psychotic, but that only 10% of those not abused received such a diagnosis. Child and adolescent inpa-tients with a history positive for abuse were identified as more likely to have hallucinations than those children who were not abused (Sansonnet-Hayden, Haley, Marriage, & Fine, 1987; Famularo, Kinscherff, & Fenton, 1992). Furthermore, intrafamilial physical abuse significantly predicted paranoid symptoms of psychosis in homeless adolescents (Mundy, Robertson, Robertson, & Greenblatt, 1990). In ad-dition, research examining the severity of psychotic symptomatology delineates that symptom severity and dysfunction are positively associ-ated with abuse in patients diagnosed with schizophrenia (Lysaker et al., 2005; Schenkel, Spaulding, DiLillo, & Silverstein, 2005).

Risk and Protective Factors for the Onset of PTSD and Psychosis

A range of mediating and moderating variables that impact the ex-pression of childhood psychological disorders are replete throughout the child psychopathology literature. For example, throughout the general pediatric psychology literature, researchers have determined that children with supportive peer relationships demonstrate overall better adjustment to their chronic illnesses and associated complicated medical regiments than those children without supportive peer relationships (Reiter-Purtill & Noll, 2003). Greco, Shroff Pendely, McDonell, & Reeves (2001) conducted a study in which they demonstrated increased medical adherence to diabetes regiments in adolescents by including their best friends in the intervention. While peer relationships are believed to enhance adjustment and coping in children in general, there is an even greater body of literature identifying family factors as impacting children's psychological well-being.

FAMILY MEDIATING AND MODERATING VARIABLES AS RISK AND PROTECTIVE FACTORS

Studies have highlighted the effectiveness of enhanced family support, adequate parent and family organization, and minimal family conflict in enhancing children's general adjustment to an array of events, including serious childhood illnesses. For example, children with spina bifida reported less cohesiveness within their families than matched samples (Holmbeck, Coakley, Hommeyer, Shapera, & Westhoven, 2002). In addition, Davis, Delamater, Shaw, LaGreca, Eidson, Perez-Reodiiques, & Nemery (2001) reported better diabetes medical adherence for children hailing from families who incorporated an authoritative parenting style (which included parenting warmth, support and control) than families without such a parenting style.

Similarly, there is a body of research regarding protective and risk factors that impact children's reactions to trauma. Some have suggested that commonly observed in abused children may be more strongly related to these risk factors than to the maltreatment experience itself (e.g., McClellan, Adams, Douglas, McCurry, & Strock, 1995). Childhood PTSD is one such disorder that is influenced greatly in its expression by mediating, risk and protective factors. Similar to patterns observed in adults, child clinicians and researchers have observed PTSD symptoms in childhood can vary notably in the severity, chronicity, and number of symptoms expressed (Faust & Furdella, 2002). These variations in symptom presentation may be the result of type of trauma itself, unique individual characteristics of the patient, and contextual events surrounding the trauma such as the ameliorating influence of social support. With respect to the latter, family variables such as family conflict, cohesion, independence, and organization have been identified in the trauma literature as influencing the psychological manifestation of child abuse (Faust & Katchen 2004). Faust and Norman-Scott (2000), discovered that the greater the family conflict and the lower the level of family organization, the more severe the trauma reaction in sexually abused children. In a different study, Faust and her colleagues found that sexually abused children's symptomatology was affected by the family environment: children from families that provided less support, were more disorganized, and did not encourage independence had children with more severe symptomatology than those children from families without these characteristics (Faust et al., 2004).

Analogous research on family-environment variables in patients with psychotic disorders has been conducted. Historically, a noxious family environment has been identified as producing significant amounts of stress for schizophrenic patients (Bateson et al., 1956; Bateson et al., 1963; Lidz & Lidz, 1949). In addition to Brown and Birley's (1968) report of increased frequency of stressful life events prior to the onset of psychotic episodes in schizophrenics, such patients are significantly more likely to relapse when exposed to psychosocial stressors, including family members who are emotionally intense and/or express critical or hostile comments (Kavanagh, 1992). Such patients are also less likely to relapse when involved in interventions designed to reduce levels of expressed emotions among family members (Hogarty et al., 1986), and psychosocial stress, such as decreasing the critical emotional reactions of their family members (Tarrier et al., 1988). Expressed emotion is a person's over involved emotional attitudes toward another person. Furthermore, research suggests a significant relationship between the severity of symptoms and stressful life events in patients with schizophrenia (Norman & Malla, 1993). Research has delineated greater levels of emotional over involvement and criticalness directed towards adult schizophrenics by their parents (Lenoir, Linszen, & Dingemans, 1998; Tompson et al., 1995).

THEORETICAL UNDERPINNINGS FOR THE DEVELOPMENT OF SCHIZOPHRENIA IN RESPONSE TO TRAUMA

Young children are more susceptible to developmental infarcts, both physical and environmental, than older children and adults. This is consistent with findings from Fletcher's (1996) meta-analytic study on youth exposed to a traumatic event, which reported average incidence rates of posttraumatic stress disorder (PTSD) as follows: 39% of pre-schoolers, 33% of elementary school children, and 27% of adolescents. It is also likely that the impact of trauma may have greater deleterious consequences for the very young. One of the core premises of psychodynamic theory regarding the etiology of thought disorders is based in developmental disruptions occurring early on in life. The section to follow will elucidate the contributions of psychodynamic theory with respect to development and attachment regarding the development of psychotic symptoms.

Attachment is primed to occur in sequential development that coincide with Melanie Klein's (1946) paranoid-schizoid position and W. R. D. Fairbairn's (1940, 1941) schizoid position. During these early stages of development the infant experiences psychotic anxieties, primitive forms of defense mechanisms and early object relations, with the first object being the "mother's breast" (feeding events) which sometimes is gratifying and other times is frustrating (a severance of love and hate; Klein, 1946). Consequently the object is split into good and bad objects and become introjected as well as projected. Frustrating object relations result in concomitant destructive impulses for all infants and while the first oral sadistic attack may be fantasized towards the breast or breast representatives such fantasized impulses evolve to include the destruction of the primary caregiver's entire body (Klein, 1946). These anhilistic impulses toward mother or her representative can engender persecutory fears to such an extreme that the infant believes he or she will be retaliated against by being destroyed directly or indirectly via abandonment (Klein, 1946). It is impossible to prevent some bad object interactions due to the course of life. For example by the time the child signals he or she has a wet diaper during his or her nap, the discomfort has already occurred; hence the infant has had a negative object experience. It is the number of these experiences and the response the primary caregiver emits to reduce the bad object that impacts the quality of ego development and attachment. Furthermore, the manner in which the mother or primary caregiver responds to the anhilistic rage of the infant will either delimit or enhance the child's sense of fear regarding retaliatory anhilistic behaviors on the part of the mother. In fact, according to Klein (1946), if the persecutory fears are extremely strong and unremitting, it may be difficult for the infant to work through the paranoid-schizoid position and may "strengthen the fixation-points for severe psychosis" (p. 15). Klein (1946) also believed another deleterious outcome of unremitting persecutory anxiety during this time is the individual may be at risk for developing bipolar disorder.

Hence it is not surprising that the introjection and projection of bad objects which in turn contributes to fantasized destructive impulses of mother, by child, leads the child to believe the mother or mother surrogate will persecute him or her. This process will impact the child's behavior which alternately demands a response from the mother. The quality of attachment is determined by these interactions. Winnicott (1965) postulated that to have healthy intrapsychic development the child must incorporate many more positive object relations than bad, which is the cornerstone of the "good enough" parenting required for healthy development to occur. It is likely then that disruptions in the quality of attachment through egregious and continuous errors in parenting and/or early trauma could result in the psychotic fixation to which Melanie Klein (1946) referred.

Harry Stack Sullivan's preverbal infancy period is characterized by difficulty thinking about events and understanding stimuli and events, as well as difficulty communicating these experiences to others (Arieti, 1974). Thus, due to the infant's inability to verbalize their experiences, the young infant is at risk in their ability to seek out satisfaction of his or her needs and to process conflicting and confusing events and stimuli. Hence traumatized infants are at greater risk for maladjustment since their experience of the trauma may remain disorganized and unprocessed. It has been postulated that the positive symptoms of schizophrenia are expressions of primitive affect experienced in infancy, reexperienced in adulthood. These affective expressions are the fragmented experiences of the preverbal infant.

There are data to indicate that disruptions in attachment formation, an inability to process emotional information, and the use of disorganized coping strategies are more likely to develop when a young child experiences a significant trauma such as physical or sexual abuse (Emanuel, 1996; Lyons-Ruth & Block, 1996.) The younger the child is when a trauma such as abuse occurs, the more likely disruptions in development will occur. These disruptions will severely negatively impact behavior and social development. Research has demonstrated serious impairment in children's attachment when exposed to early maltreatment (Fish & Chapman, 2004). In fact, over the years Ainsworth added a fourth type of attachment to the original three in order to account for the attachment patterns observed in children exposed to maltreatment. This fourth type, called the disorganized/disoriented, is a combination of two of the previous attachment patterns identified by Ainsworth: anxious resistant and anxious avoidant.

The trauma of loss of primary caretakers in infancy has also been associated with disordered attachment. For example foster care research has identified reactive attachment problems in infants and small children as being prevalent in this population (Fish & Chapman, 2004). Other research has demonstrated disruptions in attachment such as overclinginess and separation anxiety in young children traumatized by terrorism. The Oklahoma City bombings contributed to infants being more irritable and difficult to soothe by their primary caretakers (Pfefferbaum et al., 1999). Reynolds (2005) reported that infant depression is related to trauma and attachment disruptions. Hence, it may be the timing of extreme forms of parenting or interpersonal events (i.e. abuse) that impact symptom presentation.

Patterson, Birchwood and Cochrane (2005) discovered that among first episode schizophrenics and their primary caregivers perceived loss was related to high emotional over-involvement and criticalness. Similarly, Willinger, Heiden, Meszaros, Formann, and Aschauer, (2002) also discovered that schizophrenics and those with schizoaffective disorder rated their mothers as less caring and more overprotective on the parental bonding instrument than their non-diagnosed siblings. There was a significant relationship with maternal bonding and premorbid personality traits suggesting the interactive nature of attachment between child and caregiver in families with schizophrenic children. Bell and Bruscato (2002) observed in their schizophrenic sample greater levels of insecure attachment, egocentricity, and social incompetence; 85.6% of the sample exhibited some type of object relationship deficit on their measure.

Margaret Mahler's (1968) work on the relationship between mother and child, including the concepts of differentiation and hatching, also implicate the family environment as important in healthy child development. Mahler (1968) described a series of phases to explain how the child's ego gradually becomes more developed, and how the child realizes s/he is separate and distinct from his/her parents. Initially, parents serve as stimulus barriers for the infant, who has no ego of his or her own; thus, the parents protect the child from stimuli that may cause him or her to become overwhelmed. In the normal symbiotic phase, parents serve as a selective perceptive boundary, which acts as a highly selective shield and allows the child to have the rudimentary beginnings of an ego (1968). The notion of the parent's role in the protection of the child from external stimuli that may cause him to become anxious or overwhelmed may have implications for the development of psychosis. For instance, parents may fail to provide children with such protection and as a result, the child may have difficulty modulating sensory stimuli or regulating emotions later in developmental sequence. Mahler (1968) suggested that a satisfying symbiotic phase allows the child to successfully disengage from his primary caretakers during the separation and individual phase of development. It is possible that child sexual or physical abuse early on overwhelms the child's developing ego. In addition, while children with secure attachments feel comfortable using parents as a secure base to explore their surroundings, abused children, may not feel sufficiently secure in their attachments to explore. Such exploration is important because it allows children to realize they are separate and distinct from their parents, which allows them to become more independent. Thus, because the abused child is not likely to feel secure in his or her relationships with his parents, he or she may not feel comfortable using them as a secure base and as a result, the ground work for separation and individuation, or "hatching" has not been realized.

Research Questions

Given the theoretical predicate for the development of differential psychopathology in children, it is likely that the timing of trauma plays an essential role in the development of psychological disturbances in children. Given the literature with respect to attachment, integration and projection of object relationships as well as the research that implicates trauma histories in those with psychotic disorders, we predicted that children who experienced sexual and/or physical abuse in early childhood would be more likely to exhibit psychotic disorder symptoms than children who were traumatized in later childhood. We predicted that the children who experienced sexual and physical abuse later in their development would experience non-psychotic spectrum problems such as PTSD. In addition, given the literature on risk and protective factors predicting trauma reactions as well as the literature implicating extremely disruptive family environments in those with psychotic disorders, we hypothesized that children with psychotic disorder symptoms would hail from more conflictual families than those children with PTSD. In addition, due to the greater level of expressed emotion and reported levels of overinvolvement/overprotectiveness of primary caretakers in the schizophrenics' families, we predicted that families with children who had psychotic symptoms would perceive their families as more cohesive than non psychotic clinic referred children.

METHOD

Participants

The participants in this study were 40 children, ages six to 17 years old and their mothers or surrogate mother who received treatment from a community mental health center program specializing in child abuse. Half the sample included 20 children with the diagnosis of PTSD (mean age: 10.2 years) while the other half was comprised of 20 children with a psychotic disorder (mean age: 10.8 years), including Schizoaffective Disorder, Major Depression with Psychotic Features, or Psychotic Disorder NOS. To meet criteria for inclusion in the study, children had to have verifiable intrafamilial abuse histories (sexual, physical or both) and be living with a non-abusing custodial mother or mother surrogates. Furthermore, the offending family member(s) had to no longer be in contact with the children. Information pertaining to the temporal onset of the abuse and abuse-related variables was obtained from the state child protective agency.

Measures

Demographic Measure. A demographic information sheet was utilized to collect such information as age, race, ethnicity, characteristics of abuse (including type of abuse), age at time of abuse, and gender.

Schedule for Affective Disorders and Schizophrenia for School Age Children Epidemiological Version (K-SAS-E). The K-SADS-E (Orvaschel, 1995), a semi-structured interview used to assess lifetime and present episodes of psychiatric disorders in children, was administered to both the parent and child. The K-SADS was administered by graduate students in an American Psychological Association approved graduate school program who were reliably trained to criterion. The students were unaware of the hypotheses for this study. For the purposes of this study, the K-SADS was used as a measure of psychopathology; in order, to determine assignment to either the PTSD or psychotic symptoms group.

Family Environment Scale (FES). The Family Environment Scale (FES; Moos & Moos, 1986) is self-report measure consisting of 90 dichotomous items designed to assess the social environment characteristics of families. The measure is completed by the mother or female caregiver to assess perceptions of family social interactions; in addition, children over the age of 12 completed the FES, while children younger than 12 completed the Children's Version of the Family Environment Scale (Pino, Simons, & Slawinowski, 1984) The FES is comprised of 10 scales grouped into 3 domains of family functioning. Within the Relationship Domain, three scales measure Cohesion, Expressiveness, and Conflict. In the Personal Growth Domain, five scales measure Independence, Achievement Orientation, Intellectual-Cultural Orientation, Active-Recreational Orientation, and Moral Religious Emphasis. Finally, the two scales comprising the System Maintenance Domain are Organization and Control. Alpha coefficients for each of the ten scales ranged from .67 to .78 (Moos, 1990); the Cohesion and Conflict scales have been reported to have alpha coefficients of .69 and.70, respectively (Sanford, Bingham, & Zucker, 1999). In this study, the family cohesion (amount of commitment and support provided within the family) and conflict (amount of openly expressed anger and conflict) were assessed. The Cohesion and Conflict scales have been shown to be highly related to other widely used measures of these constructs (Sanford et al., 1999). Higher scores indicate greater perceived family cohesion or greater perceived family conflict.

The Children's Version Family Environment Scale (CV-FES). The Children's Version Family Environment Scale (CV-FES; Pino et al., 1984) is a 30-item pictorial scale used to assess 5-12 year old children's perceptions of the family and social climate. This measure is comprised of 10 scales depicting three domains of family's functioning and environment identical to those found on the Family Environment Measure (Moos & Moos, 1986). To complete the measure children were asked to choose one of three pictures to best describe their family across a variety of domains. The measure has a 4-week test-retest reliability of .80. In the present study, both family cohesion (amount of commitment and support provided within the family) and conflict (amount of openly expressed anger and conflict) were assessed. Higher scores indicate greater cohesiveness or greater conflict.

Procedure

After informed consent was obtained, and prior to receiving treatment, the K-SADS-E, FES, and CV-FES were administered independently to maternal figure and child by trained doctoral level students who were blind to the hypothesis of the study. Once diagnosed by the K-SADS-E, the children were divided into two groups of continuous admissions to the clinic. Once one group of 20 children had been en-rolled, the second group received subjects until the quota of 20 was met.

RESULTS

First, correlation analyses did not reveal significant differences be-tween measures and potential nuisance variables including age and gen-der. Next t tests were performed to compare the two diagnostic groups of children (psychotic symptoms vs. PTSD) with respect to the variable, age at onset of trauma exposure. Results indicated that children with psychotic disorders first experienced trauma at a mean age of 58.65 months, while children with PTSD first experienced trauma at a mean age of 94.95 months. Analysis revealed that the onset of trauma was sig-nificantly different for these two groups, $t(38) = 2.42$, $p < .02$. Table 1 il-lustrates the mean age of trauma onset as well as standard deviations and ranges for both groups.

Next, the data were analyzed to compare family members' perceived level of family conflict and cohesion between the two groups. With re-spect to children's perception of family environment, children with psy-chotic disorders reported significantly more familial conflict than children with PTSD, $t(36) = 2.09$, $p < .04$. However, there were no sig-nificant differences between children with psychotic disorders and those diagnosed with PTSD regarding perceived family cohesiveness. With respect to mothers' perceptions of family environment, when compared to mothers of children with PTSD, mothers of psychotic chil-dren rated their family as less cohesive, $t(33) = 2.19$, $p < .03$ and demon-strated a trend towards greater family conflict, $t(33) = 1.93$, $p < .06$. Table 2 illustrates means, standard deviations, and ranges for all mothers' and their children's family conflict and cohesion scores.

DISCUSSION

Results indicated that children with psychotic disorders first experi-enced trauma at a mean age of 4 years, 9 months, while children with PTSD first experienced trauma at a mean age of 7 years, 9 months. This finding is consistent with the literature indicating that earlier adverse events may be more detrimental to children's mental health than trau-matic events occurring later in childhood, due to the developmental ef-fects of traumatic stress on the developing child. Such a finding is

TABLE 1. Age of Abuse in Months (m)

Group	Mean Age	SD	Range
Psychotic	58.65 m	54 m	3-9 m
PTSD	94.95 m	39 m	30-154 m

consistent with attachment theory. It has been postulated for decades that adverse events between primary caretakers and children in early infancy renders children susceptible to the development of a psychotic disorder. Melanie Klein (1946) and Margaret Mahler (1968) postulated that the inability for primary caregivers to provide adequate mirroring and empathy of infants' sensory and feeling states as well as protection against adverse events including overwhelming stimuli results in poor attachment and integration of healthy objects.

Some of the children within the psychotic symptom group had documented histories of child abuse the first year of life; others within this group had histories occurring somewhat beyond the first year, since the mean age was reported to be around 4 and one half years of age. It is likely those children with psychotic symptoms who were abused later than one year of age and yet prior to kindergarten hailed from home environments that were maladaptive prior to the onset of abuse. Research supports the notion that abused children are more likely to have been raised in chaotic family environments prior to the commencement of the trauma (Gold, 2000). Thus in the cases of very young children who have been abused it is probable that much of their life has been spent in a disruptive home environment. In addition, it is not unusual for birth and infancy records to be unavailable to investigators as well as other professionals due to problems in record tracking, particularly in dependency cases. Consequently, much information about the child's early history is lost. Future research is warranted to more directly assess the home environments of these at-risk families throughout early development. Ideally, prospective longitudinal data should be collected from birth (or even from the prenatal period) to investigate how the family

TABLE 2. Children and Mother's Perception of Family Conflict/Cohesion as a Function of Diagnostic Group

	Mean	SD	Range
Child Report_ - Conflict			
Psychotic:	5.72	2.16	5-9
PTSD:	4.20	2.14	0-8
Mother's Report_ - Conflict			
Psychotic:	5.00	2.72	2-9
PTSD:	3.39	2.20	0-8
Child Report_ - Cohesion			
Psychotic:	5.17	2.26	0-9
PTSD:	6.10	2.13	2-9
Mother's Report_ - Cohesion			
Psychotic:	5.47	2.70	0-9
PTSD:	7.11	1.64	4-8

milieu of children who eventually are abused differs from that of those who do not experience such adversity.

In our study, abused children with psychotic symptoms reported more familial conflict than children with PTSD. This supports the concept that individuals with psychotic symptomatology hail from highly disruptive families. Peterson and Docherty (2005) found that parents of adult children with schizophrenia were more controlling of their children if they were high in expressed emotion. Lenoir and colleagues (1998) found that schizophrenics were likely to relapse more often when their mothers' level of criticalness was high on a measure of expressed emotion. There is some research which suggests that high criticalness is linked to the parents' beliefs that psychotic symptoms are under the child's control (Weisman, Nuechlerlein, Goldstein, & Snyder, 1998). Perhaps parents of children with PTSD tend to externalize the locus of control of symptomatology whereas those of psychotic symptomatology tend to internalize symptoms (i.e. believing symptoms are under the volition of the patient) which increase the parents' expectations and concomitant criticalness, leading to greater family conflict. With respect to parents' expectations and criticalness, Lenoir and colleagues (1998) observed greater dissatisfaction of parents of schizophrenics who relapsed than those who did not. While in the present study, mothers of children with psychotic symptoms were not significantly different from those mothers with children with PTSD regarding their perception of family conflict, the trend did indicate mothers of the former group perceived greater family conflict than the mothers with PTSD children. A replication of this study with a greater number of subjects could assist in elucidating the integrity of this trend prior to concluding the existence of such a relationship.

In comparison to mothers of children with PTSD, mothers of psychotic children rated their family as less cohesive. This may be due to the fact that mothers of individuals with psychotic symptomatology are primed towards a higher expectation for family cohesiveness with the identified child as evidenced by research which indicates greater emotional over involvement and overprotectiveness on the part of these parents. It has been reported that individuals with schizoaffective disorder viewed their mothers as more overprotective than their non-diagnosed siblings (Willinger et al., 2002). It also may be that the measure of cohesiveness pertains to healthy attachment instead of emotional overprotectiveness/enmeshment. As previously reviewed, the literature indicates that those with a psychotic disorder have had disruptions in attachment with primary caregivers (e.g., Karon & Vandenbos, 1994; Klein, 1946; Mahler, 1968); given these disruptions, it follows that these mothers would feel less cohesion with their children and other family members. Additionally, the literature is replete with studies which indicate living with a person with serious mental illness can contribute to family chaos. It follows then that this disruptiveness or chaos can adversely impact family cohesiveness.

Within the dyads, the perspective of children with psychotic disorders of their home environment differs in part from their mothers such that the children with psychotic symptoms viewed the family as having greater conflict than the children with PTSD whereas the mothers of the former child group only reported a trend in this direction. Mothers of psychotic disordered children perceived their families as significantly less cohesive than mothers of PTSD children. It may be that children with psychotic symptoms are responding differentially from their mothers to the home environment. It also may be that the mothers' emphasis on cohesiveness and protection is experienced as aversive on the part of the patient. This aversiveness renders the psychotic child's perception of their home environment as conflictual. As stated earlier the overprotection and controlling behavior noted by researchers leads to greater emotional over involvement and criticalness on part of the parent (Lenoir et al., 1998; Weisman et al., 1998).

Since this is a preliminary study, future research is needed to expand upon and replicate the current findings. Measures from multiple respondents as well as other measures than the ones utilized to assess family conflict and cohesion should be used. In addition, perhaps a better measure of family environment for these populations should include an assessment of family independence and its relationship to the family environment overall, including conflict and enmeshment.

REFERENCES

Arieti, S. (1974). *The interpretation of schizophrenia* (2nd ed.). New York: Basic Books.

Asarnow, J. R., Asarnow, R. F., Hornstein, N., & Russell, A. (1991). Child-onset schizophrenia: Developmental perspectives on schizophrenic disorders. In E.F. Walker (Ed.), *Schizophrenia: A life course developmental perspective. Personality, psychopathology and psychotherapy series.* San Diego, CA: Academic Press Inc.

Bateson, G., Jackson, D. D., Haley, J., & Weakland, J. (1956). Toward a theory of schizophrenia. *Behavioral Science, 1,* 251-264.

Bateson, G., Jackson, D. D., & Weakland, J. (1963). A note on the double-bind -1962. *Family Process, 2,* 154-163.

Bell, M., & Bruscato, W. (2002). Object relations deficits in schizophrenia: A cross-cultural comparisons between Brazil and the United States. *Journal of Nervous and Mental Disease, 190,* 73-79.

Brown, G. W., & Birley, J. L. T. (1968). Crisis and life change and the onset of schizophrenia. *Journal of Health and Social Behavior, 9,* 203-214.

Browne, A., & Finkelhor, D. (1986). Impact of child sexual abuse. *Psychological Bulletin, 99,* 66-77.

Davis, C.,Delamater, A., Shaw, K., LaGreca, A., Eidson, M., Perez-Reodiiques, J., & Nemery, R. (2001). Brief Report: Parenting styles, regimen adherence, and glycemic control in 4-10 year old children with diabetes. *Journal of Pediatric Psychology, 25,* 69-77.

Deblinger, E., McLeer, S., Atkins, M., Ralphe, D., & Foa, E. (1989). Post-traumatic stress in sexually abused, physically abused, and nonabused children. *Child Abuse and Neglect, 13,* 403-408.

Emanuel, R. (1996). Psychotherapy with children traumatized in infancy. *Journal of Child Psychotherapy, 22,* 214-239.

Fairbairn, W. R. D. (1940). *Schizoid Factors in Personality. An object relations theory of the personality.* New York: Basic Books (1952).

Fairbairn, W. R. D (1941). *A revised psychopathology of the psychoses and psychoneuroses. An object relations theory of the personality.* New York: Basic Books (1952).

Famularo, R. A, Kinscherff, R. T., & Fenton, T. (1992). Psychiatric Diagnoses of Maltreated Children. *Journal of American Academy of Child and Adolescent Psychiatry, 31,* 863-867.

Faust, J., & Katchen, L. B. (2004). Treatment of children with complicated posttraumatic stress reactions. *Psychotherapy: Theory, Research, Practice, Training, 21,* 426-437.

Faust, J., & Furdella, J. (2002, April). Trauma symptoms in sexually abused children: the impact of development. Paper presented at the annual meeting of the American Psychological Association, Chicago, IL.

Faust, J., Furdella, J., & Villa, M. (2004). Trauma symptoms in sexually abused children: Risk and Protective Factors. Paper presented at the annual meeting of the American Psychological Association, Honolulu, Hawaii.

Fish, B., & Chapman, B. (2004). Mental health risks to infants and toddlers in foster care. *Clinical Social Work Journal, 32* (2), 121-140.

Faust, J. & Norman-Scott, D. (2000, November). Risk and protective factors in the trauma response to childhood sexual abuse trauma. Paper presented at the annual meeting of the Association for the Advancement of Behavior Therapy. New Orleans, LA.

Fletcher, K. E. (1996). Childhood posttraumatic stress disorder. In E. J. Mash & R. A. Barkley (Eds.), *Child psychopathology* (pp. 242-275). New York: Guilford.

Freud, S. (1911). Psychoanalytic notes upon an autobiographical account of a case of paranoia (dementia paranoides). In S. Freud, *Three Case Histories.* New York: Collier Books.

Fromm-Reichmann, F. (1948). Notes on the development of treatment of schizophrenics by psychoanalytic psychotherapy. *Psychiatry: Interpersonal & Biological Processes, 11,* 263-273.

Gold, S. (2000). *Not trauma alone.* Philadelphia, PA. Brunner-Routledge.

Goldberg, J. F., & Garno, J. L. (2005). Development of posttraumatic stress disorder in adult bipolar patients with histories of severe childhood abuse. *Journal of Psychiatric Research, 39,* 595-601.

Greco, P., Shroff Pendley, J., McDonell, K., & Reeves, G. (2001). A peer group intervention for adolescents with type 1 diabetes and their best friends. *Journal of Pediatric Psychology, 26,* 485-490.

Hall, D. K. (1999). "Complex" posttraumatic stress disorder/disorders of extreme stress (CP/DES) in sexually abused children: An exploration study. *Journal of Child Sexual Abuse, 8,* 51-71.

Hogarty, G.E., Anderson, C.M., Reiss, D.J., Kornblith, S.J., Greenwald, D.P., Javna, C.D., et al. (1986). Family psychoeducation, social skills training and maintenance of chemotherapy in the aftercare treatment of schizophrenia. I: One-year effects of a controlled study on relapse and expressed emotion. *Archives of General Psychiatry 43,* 633-642.

Holmbeck, G. N., Coakley, R. M., Hommeyer, J. S., Shapera, W. E., & Westhoven, V. C. (2002). Observed and perceived dyadic & systemic functioning in families of preadolescents with spina bifida. *Journal of Pediatric Psychology, 27,* 177-189.

Kaplan, H. I., Sadock, B. J., & Grebb J. A. (1994). *Kaplan and Sadock's synopsis of psychiatry: Behavioral sciences, clinical psychiatry (7th edition).* Baltimore, MD: Williams & Wilkins Co.

Karon, B., & Vandenbos, G. (1994). *Psychotherapy of Schizophrenia: The Treatment of Choice.* Northvale, N.J.: Jason Aronson Press.

Kavanagh, D. (1992). Recent developments in expressed emotion and schizophrenia. *British Journal of Psychiatry, 160,* 601-602.

Klein, M. (1946). *Notes on some schizoid mechanism. Envy and gratitude and other works* (1946-1963). New York: Delacorte Press, 1975.

LaGreca, A. M., Silverman, W. K., Vernberg, E. M., & Prinstein, M. J. (1996). Symptoms of posttraumatic stress in children after Hurricane Andrew: A prospective study. *Journal of Consulting and Clinical Psychology, 64,* 712-723.

La Greca, A.M., Silverman, W. K., Vernberg, E.M., & Roberts, M.C. (2002). (Eds.), *Helping children cope with disasters.* Washington, DC: American Psychological Association.

Lenoir, M. E., Linszen,D. H., & Dingemans, P.M. (1998). The association between parental expressed emotion and psychotic relapse: Applying a quantitative measure for expressed emotion. *International Clinical Pharmacology, 13,* 81-87.

Lidz, R. W., & Lidz, T (1949). The family environment of schizophrenic patients. *American Journal of Psychiatry, 106,* 332-345.

Livingston, R. (1987). Sexually and physically abused children. *Journal of the American Academy of Child and Adolescent Psychiatry, 26,* 413-415.

Lyons-Ruth, K., & Block, D. (1996). The disturbed caregiving system: Relations among childhood trauma, maternal caregiving, and infant affect and attachment. *Infant Mental Health Journal, 17,* 257-275.

Lysaker, P. H, Beattie, N. L., Strasburger, A. M., & Davis, L. W. (2005). Reported history of child sexual abuse in schizophrenia: Associations with heightened symptom levels and poorer participation over four months in vocational rehabilitation. *Journal of Nervous Mental Disease, 193,* 790-795.

Mahler, M. (1968). *On Human Symbiosis and the Vicissitudes of Individuation.* New York, NY: International Universities Press.

McClellan, J., Adams, J., Douglas, D., McCurry, C., & Storck, M. (1995). Clinical characteristics related to severity of sexual abuse: A study of seriously mentally ill youth. *Child Abuse and Neglect, 19,* 1245-1254.

McLeer, S. V., Deblinger, E., Atkins, M. S., & Foa., E. B (1988). Post-traumatic stress disorder in sexually abused children. *Journal of the American Academy of Child and Adolescent Psychiatry, 27,* 650-654.

Meston, C. M., Rellini, A. H., & Heiman, J. R. (2006). Women's history of sexual abuse, their sexuality and sexual self. *Journal of Consulting and Clinical Psychology, 74,* 229-236.

Moos, R.H. (1990). Conceptual and empirical approaches to developing family based assessment procedures: Resolving the case of the Family Environment Scale. *Family Process, 29,* 199-208.

Moos, R.H. & Moos, B.S. (1986). *Family environment scale manual* (2nd ed.). Palo Alto, California: Consulting Psychologists Press, Inc.

Mundy, P., Robertson, M., Robertson, K., & Greenblatt, M. (1990). The prevalence of psychotic symptoms in homeless adolescents. *Journal of the American Academic of Child and Adolescent Psychiatry, 29,* 724 - 731.

Norman, R. M., & Malla, A. K. (1993). Stressful life events and schizophrenia: I. A review of the research. *British Journal of Psychiatry, 162,* 161-166.

Orvaschel, H. (1995). *The schedules for affective disorders and schizophrenia for school age children, epidemiological version.* Unpublished manuscript: Fort Lauderdale, FL, Nova Southeastern University.

Patterson, P., Birchwood, M., & Cochrane, R. (2005). Expressed emotion as an adaptation to loss: Prospective study in first episode psychosis. *British Journal of Psychiatry, 187,* 59-64.

Peterson, E. C., & Docherty, N. M. (2005). Expressed emotion, attribution, and control in parents of schizophrenic patients. *Psychiatry: Interpersonal and Biological Processes, 67,* 197-202.

Pfefferbaum, B., Nixon, S., Tucker, P. M., Tivis, R. D. Moore, V. L., Gurwitch, R. H. et al. (1999). Posttraumatic stress responses in bereaved children after the Oklahoma City bombing. *Journal of the American Academy of Child and Adolescent Psychiatry, 38,* 1372-1379.

Pino, C. J., Simon, N., & Slawinowski, M. J. (1984*). The children's version of the family environment scale manual.* East Aurora, New York: Slosson Educational Publications, Inc.

Read, J., Van Os, J., Morrison, A. P., & Ross, C. A. (2005). Childhood trauma, psychosis and schizophrenia: A literature review with theoretical and clinical implications. *Acta Psychiatrica Scandinavica, 112,* 330-350.

Reiter-Purtill, J., & Noll, R. B. (2003). Peer Relationships of Children with Chronic Illness. In Roberts, Michael, C. (Ed). *Handbook of Pediatric Psychology (3rd edition).*

Reynolds, G. P. (2005). Developmental Psychobiology. *American Journal of Psychiatry, 162,* 409-410.

Sanford, K. Bingham, C. R., & Zucker, R. A. (1999). Validity issues with the Family Environment Scale: Psychometric resolution and research applications with alcoholic families. *Psychological Assessment, 11,* 315-325.

Sansonnet-Hayden, H., Haley, G., Marriage, K., & Fine, S. (1987) Sexual abuse and psychopathology in hospitalized adolescents. *Journal of the American Academy of Child and Adolescent Psychiatry, 26,* 753-757.

Schenkel, L. S., Spaulding, W.D., DiLillo, D., & Silverstein, S. M. (2005). Histories of childhood maltreatment in schizophrenia: relationships with premorbid functioning, symptomatology, and cognitive deficits. *Schizophrenia Research, 76,* 273-286.

Stovall-McClough, K., & Cloitre, M. (2006) Unresolved attachment, PTSD, and dissociation in women with child abuse histories. *Journal of Consulting and Clinical Psychology, 74,* 219-228.

Tarrier, N., Barrowclough, C., Vaughn, C., Bamrah, J. S., Porceddu, K., Watts, S. & Freeman, H. (1988). The community management of schizophrenia: A controlled trial of a behavioral intervention with families to reduce relapse. *British Journal of Psychiatry, 153,* 532-542.

Tompson, M. C., Goldstein, M. J., Lebell, M. B., Mintz, L. I., Marder, S. R., & Mintz, J. (1995). Schizophrenic patient's perceptions of their relatives attitudes. *Psychiatry Research, 57,* 155-167.

Tremblay, C., Hebert, M., & Piche, C. (2000). Type I and type II posttraumatic stress disorder in sexually abused children. *Journal of Child Sexual Abuse, 9,* 65-90.

Volkmar, F.R. (1996). Child and adolescent psychosis: A review of the past ten years. *Journal of the American Academy of Child and Adolescent Psychiatry, 35,* 843-851.

Weisman, A. G., Nuechlerlein, K. H., Goldstein, M. J., & Snyder, K. S. (1998). Expressed emotion, attributions, and schizophrenia symptom dimensions. *Journal of Abnormal Psychology, 107,* 355-359.

Willinger, U., Heiden, A. M., Meszaros, K., Formann, A. K., & Aschauer, H. N. (2002). Maternal bonding behavior in schizophrenia and schizoaffective disorders, considering premorbid personality traits. *Australian and New Zealand Journal of Psychiatry, 36,* 663-668.

Winnicott, D.W.(1965). *Maturational process and the facilitating environment: Studies in the theory of emotional development.* New York: International Universities Press.

Wolfe, V. Gentile, C., & Wolfe, D. (1989). The impact of sexual abuse on children: A PTSD formulation. *Behavior Therapy, 20,* 215-228.

doi:10.1300/J513v06n02_05

Gender Differences in Relationship Patterns Between Adverse Psychiatric Experiences, Lifetime Trauma, and PTSD

Anouk L. Grubaugh
Karen J. Cusack
Eunsil Yim
Rebecca G. Knapp
B. Christopher Frueh

Anouk L. Grubaugh, PhD, is affiliated with the Department of Psychiatry and Behavioral Sciences, Medical University of South Carolina, Charleston, SC, and the Ralph H. Johnson Veterans Affairs Medical Center, Charleston, SC.

Karen J. Cusack, PhD, is Postdoctoral Fellow, Cecil G. Sheps Center for Health Services Research, University of North Carolina at Chapel Hill, Chapel Hill, NC (E-mail: kcusack@schsr.unc.edu).

Eunsil Yim, MS, is Biostatistician, Biostatistics, Bioinformatics & Epidemiology, Medical University of South Carolina, Charleston, SC (E-mail: yim@musc.edu).

Rebecca G. Knapp, PhD, is Professor, Biostatistics, Bioinformatics & Epidemiology, Medical University of South Carolina, Charleston, SC (E-mail: knappr@musc.edu).

B. Christopher Frueh, PhD, is affiliated with the Department of Psychiatry and Behavioral Sciences, Medical University of South Carolina, Charleston, SC, and the Ralph H. Johnson Veterans Affairs Medical Center, Charleston, SC (E-mail: fruehbc@musc).

Please address correspondence to: Anouk L. Grubaugh, PhD, Medical University of South Carolina, Division of Public Psychiatry, Department of Psychiatry and Behavioral Sciences, 67 President Street, P.O. Box 250861, Charleston, SC 29425 (E-mail: grubaugh@musc.edu).

[Haworth co-indexing entry note]: "Gender Differences in Relationship Patterns Between Adverse Psychiatric Experiences, Lifetime Trauma, and PTSD." Grubaugh et al. Co-published simultaneously in *Journal of Psychological Trauma* (The Haworth Maltreatment & Trauma Press, an imprint of The Haworth Press) Vol. 6, No. 2/3, 2007, pp. 87-98; and: *Trauma and Serious Mental Illness* (ed: Steven N. Gold, and Jon D. Elhai) The Haworth Maltreatment & Trauma Press, an imprint of The Haworth Press, 2007, pp. 87-98. Single or multiple copies of this article are available for a fee from The Haworth Document Delivery Service [1-800-HAWORTH, 9:00 a.m. - 5:00 p.m. (EST). E-mail address: docdelivery@haworthpress.com].

SUMMARY. We examined the interrelationships between gender, adverse psychiatric experiences, lifetime trauma, and PTSD among severely mentally ill patients via secondary analyses. Participants were 142 adult, psychiatric patients, randomly-selected from a public-sector setting. They completed self-report measures to assess for victimization during the course of their psychiatric care, lifetime victimization, and PTSD. There were a number of significant associations between psychiatric and lifetime victimization experiences among both men and women. However, victimization within the psychiatric setting was not significantly related to PTSD for either men or women. Replication and expansion of these findings is encouraged to promote safety in psychiatric settings. doi:10.1300/J513v06n02_06 *[Article copies available for a fee from The Haworth Document Delivery Service: 1-800-HAWORTH. E-mail address: <docdelivery@haworthpress.com> Website: <http://www.HaworthPress.com> © 2007 by The Haworth Press, Inc. All rights reserved.]*

KEYWORDS. Trauma, PTSD, psychiatric patients, gender, psychiatric experiences

Although there is a growing body of data indicating high rates of both lifetime trauma and posttraumatic stress disorder (PTSD) among individuals with severe mental illness (SMI) (Mueser et al., 1998; Switzer et al., 1999), little is known regarding the frequency and consequences of traumatic events occurring in this population *within* public psychiatric settings (Frueh et al., 2000). To date, two studies have reported on the frequency of a wide range of both harmful and traumatic experiences occurring during the course of psychiatric care; and each study found high rates of both (Cusack, Frueh, Hiers, Suffoletta-Maierle, & Bennett, 2003; Frueh et al., 2005). More specifically, In these two studies involving mental health consumers served by the South Carolina public mental health system (1) 86% and 82% reported institutional events and procedures such as handcuffed transport or restraints; (2) 44% and 40% reported sexual or physical assault; (3) 39% and 46% reported use of coercive measures; (4) 26% and 63%; reported witnessing traumatic events; and (5) 23% and 42% reported verbal intimidation or abuse respectively. Furthermore, the occurrence of these traumatic and harmful events was significantly associated with subjective ratings of distress. Due to the frequency with which these patients reported a wide range of harmful and traumatic events during the course of their psychiatric care, further examination of variables that may potentially be related to both the occurrence and the perceived distress of these experiences is needed. One relevant variable is gender, which is known to be a significant factor in the epidemiology of both trauma and PTSD (Kessler, Sonnega, Bromet, Hughes, & Nelson, 1995).

In the general population, rates of trauma exposure are typically higher for men than for women. For example, Kessler and colleagues (1995) found that 61% of men and 51% of women reported at least one traumatic event in their lifetime. Similarly, another study found that men reported an average of 5.3 distinct traumas whereas the number reported by women averaged 4.3 (Breslau et al., 1998). In another study, 55% of men compared to 46% of women reported experiencing multiple traumatic events (Stein, Walker, Hazen, & Forde, 1997). Although these studies seem to indicate that men experience more trauma than do women, they also reveal that women are more likely than men to experience certain forms of trauma such as sexual victimization. Furthermore, women are more likely than men to develop PTSD following exposure to a traumatic event, with a 2:1 ratio regardless of base rates of trauma exposure (Breslau et al., 1998; Kessler et al., 1995).

Studies of patients with SMI, who are served in public psychiatric settings, have not typically yielded differential rates of overall trauma exposure and PTSD by gender (Cascardi, Mueser, DeGiralomo, & Murrin, 1996; Cusack, Frueh, & Brady, 2004; Mueser et al., 1998; Mueser et al., 2004; Switzer et al., 1999). However, like women in the general population, women with SMI are more likely to be sexually assaulted (Cusack et al., 2004; Mueser et al., 1998; Mueser et al., 2004; Switzer et al., 1999) and are at a greater risk for developing PTSD when exposed to a traumatic event (Mueser et al., 2004). Together, these findings indicate that men and women with and without SMI are at risk for experiencing different types of trauma, and women appear more susceptible to the negative effects of these experiences. These data suggest the possibility that the frequency and experience of particular traumatic events within the psychiatric setting, such as physical and sexual victimization, may be different for men and women.

Our own recent work did not reveal statistically significant differences in the proportion of male and female patients endorsing any of a wide range of individual types of traumatic or harmful psychiatric experiences (Cusack, Grubaugh, Knapp, & Freuh, 2006). However, our prior analyses did not specifically examine the interrelationship between gender, victimization experiences, lifetime trauma, and PTSD within psychiatric settings. Therefore, the current study represents a more thorough examination of the data from the original project, without replicating prior analyses, having the purpose of better understanding the differential experience of physical and/or sexual victimization within psychiatric settings among male and female public sector patients. We specifically report secondary analyses on the interrelationships between gender, and physical and sexual victimization, lifetime physical and sexual victimization, and PTSD. We hope that these findings will stimulate a discussion regarding the differential experiences of men and women within psychiatric settings and will lay the foundation for future *a priori* hypothesis-confirming studies on this important topic.

METHOD

Participants

Study participants were 142 randomly-selected, volunteer, male and female patients (age > 18), from a Charleston day-hospital program affiliated with the South Carolina Department of Mental Health (SCDMH). Patients in the SCDMH have SMI such as schizophrenia, bipolar disorder, and/or major depressive disorder; and they require assistance with independent living skills, symptom management, and pre-vocational skills. Many have had multiple psychiatric hospitalizations, both voluntary and involuntary. Patients receive continuous medication management and support services to prevent the recurrence of severe symptoms of mental illness. Over 100 consumers attend daily and are involved in the program long-term.

Between 2002 and 2004, we approached 156 randomly identified potential participants, 142 of whom consented to participate, contributing a participation rate of 91.0%. Of the 14 patients who elected not to participate, 8 expressed having "no interest", 4 believed participation would be too distressing, and 2 felt their condition precluded participation. Demographics for the final sample are as follows: Mean age = 46.2 (SD = 11.6); 44.4% were female, 4.2% were married; 21.8% lived alone, 4.2% lived with a spouse, 73.9% lived with others; 76.8% had a high school education or less; 75.4% were unemployed, 0.7% worked full-time, 23.2% were Caucasian, and 76.8% were African American. The majority of the sample had a primary diagnosis of either schizophrenia (43.7%) or schizoaffective disorder (41.5%). Diagnostic information was obtained from chart review data. These demographics are generally representative of the program's clientele.

Inclusion criteria were a prior history of psychiatric hospitalization and the ability to independently and competently give informed consent. This study was conducted from 2002 to 2004 with full approval of the Institutional Review Boards of the Medical University of South Carolina and the SCDMH. All subjects signed informed consent documents prior to study participation, and were paid $25 for their participation.

Research Procedures

Participants were randomly selected from a current program roster, which was periodically updated with new admissions. A computer-generated random sampling procedure was used. Project staff approached potential participants at their scheduled visits to obtain informed consent. Patients who did not show for appointments were contacted, and arrangements were made to reschedule, if possible. All consenting subjects completed a short battery of self-report measures, which took approximately 60-90 minutes. Project staff read the self-report measures aloud to all participants in order to minimize literacy problems. A chart review of SCDMH service records was conducted for each participant to gather information on documented psychiatric diagnoses, trauma history, and past mental heath history. Diagnostic clinical and thematic interviews were also conducted on a small sub-sample, but were not included in the results presented here.

Instruments

Personal Data Sheet. This form was used to obtain information regarding demographics (i.e., age, race, gender, education, and marital status), changes in employment and marital status within 6 months of assessment, psychiatric and medical care received within 6 months of assessment, and number of arrests and changes in residential status within 12 months of assessment.

Psychiatric Experiences Questionnaire (PEQ). The PEQ, a 26-item instrument, was developed to assess for a wide range of traumatic and harmful experiences that may occur within psychiatric settings (Cusack et al., 2003; Frueh et al., 2005). PEQ items list possible experiences (e.g., being strip searched, handcuffed transport, staff name calling, sexual assault, physical assault) and assess whether events have been experienced, level of distress one week after the event (1 = "almost none" to 5 = "extreme"), and frequency of distress since the event (1 = "almost never" to 5 = "almost always"). In the present study, we limited our analyses to items on the PEQ reflecting physical and sexual victimization experiences.

Trauma Assessment for Adults-Self-Report Version (TAA). This 17-item instrument assesses for lifetime history of traumatic events and has been widely used in research on trauma exposure in adults (Resnick, 1996). Using a sample of 23 adults in a local mental health population, the authors of the TAA found that it was easy to administer (Resnick, 1996). They also found that rates of trauma and crime exposure were consistent with rates previously found in the same population using a different trauma assessment tool. Archival data from the mental health records of a subset of 15 patients revealed that the TAA detected all stressor events noted in the mental health records on these individuals, as well as others that were not. Recent data show that PTSD and trauma histories can be reliably assessed among public sector patients with SMI (Goodman et al., 1999; Mueser et al., 2001).

PTSD Checklist (PCL). The PCL is a 17-item self-report measure of PTSD symptoms based on DSM-IV criteria, with a 5-point Likert scale response format (Weathers, Litz, Herman, Huska, & Keane, 1993). Scores on the PCL range from 17 to 85, with higher scores indicating worse symptom severity. According to scoring guidelines recommended by the authors of the PCL, a cutoff score of 50 was used in the present analyses to determine PTSD diagnoses. The PCL has been found to be highly correlated with a structured interview for PTSD (r = .93). It has good diagnostic efficiency (> .70) and robust psychometric properties with a variety of trauma populations (Blanchard, Jones-Alexander, Buckley, & Forneris, 1996; Weathers et al., 1993).

Chart Review Instrument. A chart review of SCDMH records was conducted on all study participants in order to collect data on documented mental health care information over a 12-month period. The content of this instrument included documentation of: (1) psychiatric diagnoses, (2) past or current trauma history, and (3) specialty referrals, including psychiatric hospitalization.

RESULTS

We examined gender differences in sample characteristics (i.e., other demographic variables, social and occupational functioning indices, psychiatric diagnoses, and medications prescribed) using *t*-tests or Wilcoxon rank sum tests for continuous variables and chi-square or Fisher's Exact Test for dichotomous variables. In a series of gender stratified analyses, we explored the relationship between PEQ physical and sexual assault items endorsed and lifetime physical and/or sexual assaults (TAA). For men and women separately, the proportion of men and women endorsing each PEQ item were compared for those with and without a lifetime assault history using chi-square or Fisher's Exact test. Similarly, for men and women separately, the proportion of men and women endorsing each PEQ item were compared for those with and without PTSD using chi-square or Fisher's Exact test.

Gender Differences in Sample Demographic and Clinical Characteristics. First, gender differences on other demographic variables were explored. There were no significant differences between men and women on education, employment status, or living arrangement. Significant gender differences did emerge on age, marital status, and race. Specifically, female patients were older (M = 49.87 years, SD = 10.43) than male patients (M = 43.24 years, SD = 11.74), $t(140)$ = 3.51; p = .001; male patients were more likely to be single or never married than female patients, 77.2% vs. 41.3%; X^2 = 19.08, $p < .001$; and male patients were more likely to be African American than female patients, 62.4% vs. 37.6%; X^2 = 8.66, p = .003.

In comparing male and female patients on a number of social and occupational functioning indices, we found no statistically significant gender differences in the likelihood of having changed jobs, having been fired, having been married or divorced, having changed residences. In addition, we found no differences in the number of arrests within the past 12 months, or in satisfaction with the quality of one's social relationships. In terms of medical and mental healthcare visits in the past 12 months, women visited their primary care physicians more than did men, 4.46 (SD = 4.32) versus 1.49 visits (SD = 1.44), $t(44)$ = 4.14, $p < .001$. However, there were no statistically significant gender differences in the number of psychiatric or medical hospitalizations reported in the past 12 months.

Gender, PEQ Results, and TAA Categories. Table 1 presents the frequency of PEQ items by lifetime sexual and physical assault separately for men and women. Male patients who reported a sexual and/or physical assault in childhood or adulthood were more likely to report having been sexually assaulted by staff in a psychiatric setting than males without such a history. Male patients with a history of adult sexual assault were more likely to report an unwanted sexual advance and a sexual as-

TABLE 1. Endorsement of Physical and Sexual Assault Items on the Psychiatric Experience Questionnaire (PEQ) by Lifetime Sexual and Physical Assault

PEQ items	Child Sexual Abuse			Adult Sexual Assault			Physical Assault		
Males	% Yes N=15	% No N=60	p^1	% Yes N=6	% No N=69	p^1	% Yes N=37	% No N=42	p^1
Physical assault-staff	6.7	16.9	.32	33.3	14.7	.24	24.3	9.8	.08
Physical assault-patient	26.7	33.9	.59	66.7	30.9	.08	51.4	17.1	.00
Physical assault-combined	33.3	40.7	.60	60.0	38.2	.38	58.3	21.1	.00
Unwanted sexual advance	20.0	11.7	0.4	66.7	10.1	.00	21.6	9.5	.13
Sexual assault-staff	20.0	1.7	.00	66.7	0.0	.00	10.8	0.0	.03
Sexual assault-patient	13.3	8.3	.55	66.7	5.8	.00	16.2	7.1	.21
Adverse sexual experiences-combined	33.3	15.3	.14	100.0	13.2	.00	27.8	10.5	.06
Females	% Yes N=27	% No N=33	p^2	% Yes N=18	% No N=41	p^2	% Yes N=30	% No N=32	p^2
Physical assault-staff	7.4	9.1	.81	22.2	2.4	.01	10.0	6.3	.59
Physical assault-patient	18.5	18.2	.97	33.3	9.8	.03	20.0	15.6	.65
Physical assault-combined	22.2	21.2	.92	38.9	12.2	.03	25.0	18.8	.56
Unwanted sexual advance	33.3	15.2	0.1	44.4	12.2	.01	33.3	12.5	.05
Sexual assault-staff	0.0	0.0	--	0.0	0.0	--	0.0	0.0	--
Sexual assault-patient	7.4	0.0	.26	5.6	2.4	.54	6.7	0.0	.14
Adverse sexual experiences-combined	37.0	15.2	.05	44.4	14.6	.02	39.3	12.5	.02

[1] PEQ response differences among men by lifetime assault history (yes/no) using chi-square or Fisher's Exact Test

[2] PEQ response differences among women by lifetime assault history (yes/no) using chi-square or Fisher's Exact Test

sault by another patient than men without such a history. Finally, male patients with a history of physical assault were more likely to report a physical assault by another patient than those without such a history. Among female patients, women with a history of adult sexual assault were more likely to report a physical assault by staff or another patient and an unwanted sexual advance than women without such a history. Women with a history of physical assault (versus those without) also were more likely to report an unwanted sexual advance. For both men and women, the association between PEQ events endorsed and lifetime sexual and physical victimization became significant when staff and patient events were combined.

Gender, PEQ Results, and PTSD. Table 2 presents the frequency of endorsement of PEQ items by PTSD diagnosis for men and women separately. There were no statistically significant differences between those who endorsed particular PEQ items and those who did not by PTSD diagnostic status for either men or women.

DISCUSSION

With regard to demographic characteristics, male patients were younger, more likely to be single or never married, and more likely to be African American than were female patients. In terms of functioning, women visited their primary care physicians more often than did men. However, there were no statistically significant gender differences in the number of psychiatric or medical hospitalizations reported within the past 12 months. On primary outcomes, there was a significant relationship between the number of adverse psychiatric experiences and lifetime physical and sexual assault exposure for both men and women. Generally, both male and female patients with a lifetime history of sexual assault were more likely to endorse an incident of physical or sexual victimization occurring at some point during the course of their psychiatric care. For men, there was also a strong relationship between lifetime physical assault and physical assaults occurring within the psychiatric setting. For women, the strongest pattern of association was between lifetime adult sexual assault and physical assaults endorsed during the course of their psychiatric care. For men, however, lifetime sexual assault was most strongly linked to having experienced a sexual assault during the course of their psychiatric care.

Taken together, adverse psychiatric experiences for both men and women were most strongly linked with a past history of adult sexual assault. These findings are consistent with the broader re-victimization literature, which suggests that individuals with a prior history of victimization are at greater risk for experiencing another assault relative than those without such a history (Messman-Moore & Long, 2002). Furthermore, these data highlight the extreme vulnerability of individuals with SMI both within and outside of psychiatric settings and high-

TABLE 2. Endorsement of Physical and Sexual Assault Items on the Psychiatric Experience Questionnaire (PEQ) by PTSD Diagnosis

PEQ Items	Male PTSD Diagnosis			Female PTSD Diagnosis		
	PCL<50 N=69	PCL>=50 N=10	p^1	PCL<50 N=45	PCL>=50 N=17	p^2
Physical assault-staff	14.5	33.3	.15	8.9	5.9	.70
Physical assault-patient	34.8	22.2	.45	22.2	5.9	.13
Adverse sexual experiences-combined	40.6	33.3	.68	24.4	11.8	.27
Unwanted sexual advances	14.5	20.0	.65	22.2	23.5	.91
Sexual assault-staff	4.3	10.0	.45	0.0	0.0	--
Sexual assault-patient	10.1	20.0	.36	2.2	5.9	.47
Adverse sexual experiences-combined	11.6	20.0	.37	2.2	5.9	.47

[1]PEQ response differences among men by PTSD diagnosis using chi-square or Fisher's Exact Test

[2]PEQ response differences among women by PTSD diagnosis using chi-square or Fisher's Exact Test

light the need to foster patient safety in this population of trauma survivors.

There were no statistically significant differences in rates of PEQ items among the two diagnostic groups (PTSD versus no PTSD) both men or women. However, it should be noted that most patients in this sample (87%) reported a lifetime traumatic experiences (Cusack, Grubaugh, Knapp, & Frueh, 2006), and this rate of trauma may be obscuring potential differences in the relationship between endorsing sexual and physical assault items on the PEQ item and PTSD. More research along this theme is needed to better understand both the short and long term effects of sexual and physical victimization occurring within psychiatric settings.

Several study limitations merit comment. This was a cross-sectional, retrospective study that examined events occurring at *any* point during participants' lifetime, and did not specifically query for recent events. Therefore, the extent to which hospitalized patients may be currently experiencing these events is unknown. Because participants were all from a single community mental health program in the southeast, the generalizability of these findings may also be somewhat limited. Further, the data do not address causal relationships, and it is possible that some form of systematic response biases were in operation. Thus, all the caveats associated with a study of self-reported symptoms and experiences apply. Finally, due to the number of statistical comparisons made across studies (i.e., Frueh et al., 2005) and the nature of secondary analyses, the potential for family-wise error is recognized; and the present findings should be replicated using *a priori* hypothesis testing.

In summary, sexual and physical victimization within the psychiatric setting was strongly linked to lifetime victimization experiences for both men and women. Although few significant differences emerged in rates of PTSD among those who were (versus those who were not) assaulted in the psychiatric setting, these findings are potentially dampened by the high rate of lifetime trauma in this sample. Additional hypothesis-driven research is needed to replicate and extend these findings, to further enhance our understanding of issues related to gender and the impact of experiences occurring within psychiatric settings, and to improve the safety of services for both men and women served by public-sector mental health systems. It is hoped that this research will stimulate discussion and consideration of an issue that has received insufficient attention from clinicians, administrators, and policy-makers involved with mental health service delivery.

NOTE

Acknowledgement: This work was partially supported by grants MH01660 and MH65517 from the National Institute of Mental Health to Dr. Frueh.

The authors would also like to gratefully acknowledge the contributions and support for the completion of this project provided by David Sheil, MSW, Victoria Cousins, BS, Julie Sauvageot, MSW, and Thom Heirs, PhD.

REFERENCES

Blanchard E.B., Jones-Alexander J., Buckley T.C., & Forneris, C.A. (1996). Psychometric properties of the PTSD Checklist (PCL). *Behavior Research and Therapy*, 34, 669-673.

Breslau, N., Kessler, R.C., Chilcoat, H.D., Schultz, L.R., Davis, G.C., & Andreski, P. (1998). Trauma and posttraumatic stress disorder in the community: The 1996 Detroit Area Survey of Trauma. *Archives of General Psychiatry*, 55, 626-632.

Cascardi, M., Mueser, K.T., DeGiralomo, J., & Murrin, M. (1996). Physical aggression against psychiatric inpatients by family members and partners. *Psychiatric Services*, 47, 531-533.

Cusack, K.J., Frueh, B.C., & Brady, K.T. (2004). Trauma history screening in a community mental health center. *Psychiatric Services*, 55, 157-162.

Cusack, K.J., Frueh, B.C., Hiers, T., Suffoletta-Maierle, S., & Bennett, S. (2003). Trauma within the psychiatric setting: A preliminary empirical report. *Administration and Policy in Mental Health*, 30, 453-460.

Cusack, K.J., Grubaugh, A.L., Knapp, R.G., & Frueh, B.C. (2006). Unrecognized Trauma and PTSD among public mental health consumers with chronic and severe mental illness. *Community Mental Health Journal, 42,* 487-500.

Frueh, B.C., Dalton, M.E., Johnson, M.R., Hiers, T.G., Gold, P.B., Magruder, K.M., et al. (2000). Trauma within the psychiatric setting: Conceptual framework, research directions, and policy implications. *Administration and Policy in Mental Health*, 28, 147-154.

Frueh, B.C., Knapp, R.G., Cusack, K.J., Grubaugh, A.L., Sauvageot, J.A., Cousins, V.C., et al. (2005). Patients' reports of safety within the psychiatric setting. *Psychiatric Services*, 56, 1123-1133.

Goodman, L.A., Thompson, K.M., Weinfurt, K., Corl, S., Acker, P., Mueser, K.T., et al. (1999). Reliability of reports of violent victimization and posttraumatic stress disorder among men and women with serious mental illness. *Journal of Traumatic Stress*, 12, 587-599.

Kessler, R.C., Sonnega, A., Bromet, E., Hughes, M., & Nelson, C.B. (1995). Posttraumatic stress disorder in the National Comorbidity Survey. *Archives of General Psychiatry*, 52, 1048-1060.

Messman-Moore, T.L. & Long, P.J. (2002). The role of childhood sexual abuse sequelae in the sexual revictimization of women: An empirical review and theoretical reformulation. *Clinical Psychology Review*, 23, 537-571.

Mueser, K., Goodman, L.A., Trumbetta, S.L., Rosenberg, S.D., Osher, F.C., Vidaver, R., et al. (1998). Trauma and posttraumatic stress disorder in severe mental illness. *Journal of Consulting and Clinical Psychology*, 66, 493-499.

Mueser, K.T., Salyers, M.P., Rosenberg, S.D., Goodman, L.A., Essock, S.M., Osher, F.C., et al. (2004). Interpersonal trauma and posttraumatic stress disorder in patients with severe mental illness: Demographic, clinical, and health correlates. *Schizophrenia Bulletin*, 30, 45-57.

Mueser, K.T., Salyers, M.P., Rosenberg, S.D., Fox, L., Salyers, M.P., Ford, J.D., et al. (2001). Psychometric evaluation of trauma and posttraumatic stress disorder assessments in persons with severe mental illness. *Psychological Assessment*, 13, 110-117.

Resnick, H.S. (1996). Psychometric review of Trauma Assessment for Adults (TAA). In Stamm, B.H. (Ed.). *Measurement of stress, trauma, and adaptation*. Lutherville, MD: Sidran Press.

Stein, M.B., Walker, J.R., Hazen, A.L., & Forde, D.R. (1997). Full and partial posttraumatic stress disorder: Findings from a community survey. *American Journal of Psychiatry*, 154, 1114-1119.

Switzer, G.E., Dew, M.A., Thompson, K., Goycoolea, J.M., Derricott, T., & Mullins, S.D. (1999). Posttraumatic stress disorder and service utilization among urban mental health center clients. *Journal of Traumatic Stress*, 12, 25-39.

Weathers, F.W., Litz, B.T., Herman, D.S., Huska, J.A., & Keane, T.M. (1993). *The PTSD Checklist (PCL): Reliability, validity, and diagnostic utility*. Paper presented at the 9th Annual Meeting of the ISTSS, San Antonio, TX.

doi:10.1300/J513v06n02_06

CLINICAL APPLICATIONS

The Broad Relationship Between Bipolar Disorder and Disorders of Psychological Trauma– Time-Limited to Life-Long Need for Mood Stabilizers

Benjamin F. Levy

SUMMARY. This article explores the relationship between bipolar disorder and disorders of psychological trauma. While bipolar disorder is generally thought of as a life-long illness, naturalistic studies report that some patients have a self-limited course. Three patients are presented who met diagnostic criteria for bipolar disorder, responded well to mood stabilizing medication, and were subsequently able to successfully dis-

Benjamin F. Levy, MD, is Staff Psychiatrist, University Health Services, University of Massachusetts, Amherst.

Address correspondence to: Benjamin F. Levy, MD, Mental Health Clinic, University Health Services, 111 Infirmary Way, University of Massachusetts, Amherst, MA 01003 (E-mail: bfl@uhs.umass.edu).

The author would like to express gratitude to both Marlene Steinberg and Steven Gold for their encouragement and valuable feedback while writing this paper.

[Haworth co-indexing entry note]: "The Broad Relationship Between Bipolar Disorder and Disorders of Psychological Trauma–Time-Limited to Life-Long Need for Mood Stabilizers." Levy, Benjamin F. Co-published simultaneously in *Journal of Psychological Trauma* (The Haworth Maltreatment & Trauma Press, an imprint of The Haworth Press) Vol. 6, No. 2/3, 2007, pp. 99-125; and: *Trauma and Serious Mental Illness* (ed: Steven N. Gold, and Jon D. Elhai) The Haworth Maltreatment & Trauma Press, an imprint of The Haworth Press, 2007, pp. 99-125. Single or multiple copies of this article are available for a fee from The Haworth Document Delivery Service [1-800-HAWORTH, 9:00 a.m. - 5:00 p.m. (EST). E-mail address: docdelivery@haworthpress.com].

continue their mood stabilizing medication once their trauma disorder was treated and significantly improved. Other patients are presented who experienced a more persistent course of bipolar disorder. There is a literature review discussing the relationship between bipolar disorders and disorders of psychological trauma with a focus on the patients presented. Recommendations are made for clinical practice and future research. doi:10.1300/J513v06n02_07 *[Article copies available for a fee from The Haworth Document Delivery Service: 1-800-HAWORTH. E-mail address: <docdelivery@haworthpress.com> Website: <http://www.HaworthPress.com> © 2007 by The Haworth Press, Inc. All rights reserved.]*

KEYWORDS. Bipolar disorder, posttraumatic stress disorder, borderline personality disorder, dissociative disorder, complex posttraumatic stress disorder, spontaneous remission

This article will explore the relationship between bipolar disorder and disorders of psychological trauma. While bipolar disorder is generally understood as being a life-long illness requiring life-long maintenance medication (Marangell, Silver, Goff,& Yudofsky, 2003), this article will explore how this may not always be the case when bipolar disorder is co-morbid with a disorder of psychological trauma. That is, the phenotype of bipolar disorder may be present in patients with a disorder of psychological trauma (i.e. those who meet the DSM-IV criteria for bipolar disorder or the criteria for either the bipolar spectrum or bipolar spectrum disorder). However, in some of these patients, the bipolar disorder has a course that mirrors the recovery from the disorder of psychological trauma. Some patients are able to successfully discontinue their mood stabilizing medication when the disorder of psychological trauma is targeted and improves significantly or resolves. This is contrary to the current understanding of the expected course and treatment of bipolar disorder.

DIAGNOSIS AND TREATMENT OF BIPOLAR DISORDER RELATED TO PSYCHOLOGICAL TRAUMA

The American Psychiatric Association Practice Guideline describes bipolar disorder as a lifelong illness with an episodic but variable course. The Guideline further states: "at this time there is no cure for bipolar disorder; treatment can decrease associated morbidity and mortality" (American Psychiatric Association, 2000b, p. 4). It therefore recommends maintenance treatment. As such, there are no guidelines as to when to stop maintenance treatment. Therefore, most summaries of treatment for bipolar disorder include statements such as "patients with bipolar disorder require lifelong prophylaxis with a mood stabilizer, both to prevent new episodes and to decrease the likelihood that the illness will progress to a more malignant course" (Marangell et al., 2003, p. 1047). This makes sense given the ravages of social impairment, treatment resistance and suicide that can occur when mood stabilizing medication is discontinued in some patients with bipolar disorder (Jamison, 1999; Post, 2005). However, it does not make sense for those patients who have a self-limited course of bipolar disorder. The notion of bipolar disorder having a self-limited course is not discussed in the APA treatment guidelines and so it is left up to the individual patient and clinician whether to even consider struggling with the notion of discontinuing mood stabilizing medication once the diagnosis of bipolar disorder is made.

What is the mood disturbance that characterizes bipolar disorder and what is the mood disturbance that accompanies disorders of psychological trauma? Are they clearly different or are they sometimes the same? The "mood swings" of trauma disorders are treated primarily with psychotherapy, with psychopharmacology added for symptom relief. The "mood episodes" of bipolar disorder are treated primarily with psychopharmacology, with psychotherapy added to help the person adapt to and manage a chronic mental illness. Making the right diagnosis of a patient complaining of a mood disturbance–mood swings versus mood episodes–has everything to do with recommending the right treatment. Bolton and Gunderson (1996) express concern that the diagnosis of bipolar disorder in patients with borderline personality disorder may cause "the defensive use of the diagnosis and symptoms to evade responsibility." Perugi and Akiskal (2002) express concern that if bipolar disorder is distinct from borderline personality disorder, then "such a conceptualization robs 'borderline' patients from being considered as affectively ill." This article will argue that for some patients both sets of authors may be right. Some patients may be considered affectively ill (i.e., needing mood stabilizing medication), yet need to take responsibility for their symptoms (with the help of psychotherapy) and ultimately may do well enough to no longer need either psychotherapy or mood stabilizing medication.

It becomes problematic to know how to make a diagnosis and recommend treatment when the "mood swings" described in the trauma literature overlap with the "mood episodes" described in the bipolar literature. Both the nature and the duration of the symptoms can overlap. This has been described in all the disorders of psychological trauma: posttraumatic stress disorder (Lucking, 1986), borderline personality disorder (Akiskal, 2004; Akiskal, Chen, & Davis, 1985; Benazzi, 2006; Bolton & Gunderson, 1996; Henry, Mitropoulou, New, Koenigsberg, Silverman, & Siever, 2001; Paris, 2004), and dissociative disorders (Levy & Swanson, 2006, submitted for publication; Ross, 1989, Steinberg, 1995). Complex post traumatic stress disorder is a relatively new diagnostic construction and includes features of all three of the other disorders of psychological trauma.

That the symptoms themselves and their duration overlap between bipolar disorder and disorders of psychological trauma is not only a problem with DSM-IV criteria of bipolar disorder (at least four days of hypomania or seven days of mania or hospitalization); it is even more of a problem with the shorter duration criteria in bipolar spectrum disorder. The following discussion, first of the diagnosis of bipolar disorder and then of the diagnosis of disorders of psychological trauma, shows that the type and duration of mood symptoms by themselves are insufficient to decide if the patient has bipolar disorder, as we currently understand it, with the assumption that life-long mood stabilizing medication treatment is needed. This article will show that features of bipolarity (diagnostic validators, Ghaemi, 2003) such as phenomenology of manic symptoms, phenomenology of depressive symptoms, clinical course of bipolar treatment, family history, antidepressant treatment response, and mood stabilizer treatment response may help with the decision of whether to discontinue a mood stabilizer. The presence and recognition of a co-morbid trauma related disorder and the clinical course and treatment of both the bipolar disorder and the trauma related disorder together may be the most important factors in determining whether or not to continue a mood stabilizing medication for life.

PATIENT PRESENTATIONS

Patient 1

A 35 year old female diagnosed with bipolar disorder and posttraumatic stress disorder announced that she was planning to taper herself off all psychotropic medications, after over a decade of recurring psychiatric hospitalizations and intensive psychotherapy. While the patient had been doing quite well over the past two years, her clinical course had previously been quite difficult. She had been treated with a combination of lithium and various antidepressant medications for over 10 years. After a series of psychiatric hospitalizations due to either suicidal ideations or attempts, lithium was added to amitriptyline both because of a manic presentation and because of a poor response to the antidepressant medication alone. Her mother was believed to have bipolar disorder and to have benefited from lithium. Between her family history, manic and depressive presentations, and improved response when lithium was added to amitriptyline, she was diagnosed with bipolar I. Subsequently, fluoxetine was substituted for amitriptyline.

Because of recurring intrusive memories of earlier sexual abuse, withdrawn behavior, difficulty with sleep and concentration, and irritability, the diagnosis of posttraumatic stress disorder was made. She then put a tremendous effort into psychotherapy, working through her response to an unwanted sexual experience during childhood. There were several psychiatric hospitalizations because of suicide plans or out-of-control, self-destructive behaviors. With lithium and an antidepressant medication, she became euthymic with intermittent depression related to a resurgence of PTSD symptoms. Every time she tried to stop the lithium, the depression returned.

However, after 10 years of treatment, she felt very different about her earlier unwanted traumatic events. She was no longer triggered by events in her every day life. She was no longer suffering from nightmares and flashbacks. She was more comfortable engaging with peers and at work. She was no longer "on the watch" for the next bad thing to happen. She felt at peace with the world for the first time since she could remember. She felt it was time to try to go off her psychotropic medications.

I warned her that her depressions did not resolve until lithium was added and that every prior time she had tried to go off lithium there had been a depressive relapse. I further warned her that discontinuing her medications might put her at risk for treatment refractoriness (Post, Leverich, Altshuler, & Mikalauskas, 1992) and suicide (Jamison, 1999). Nonetheless, she was determined to try. First, she tapered off fluoxetine, starting at 20 mg each day and slowly decreasing the dose, over a several month period. Then, starting at lithium carbonate 900 mg at bedtime, there was a step-wise reduction of her lithium dose over several months. After being off all the medication for two years, she remained euthymic. The apparent bipolar disorder went away.

Comment. When the patient arrived for her first appointment with me, she was already taking lithium and an antidepressant medication, following a series of psychiatric hospitalizations. She met criteria for the diagnosis of bipolar I disorder and posttraumatic stress disorder. After a prolonged but successful effort in psychotherapy, her posttraumatic symptoms subsided and she was able to successfully discontinue her mood stabilizing medication. While a two year period of observation off medications may not be enough to assure a life-long freedom of mood episodes, it was dramatically different from the earlier complicated and chronic symptomatic picture. Going off and staying off mood stabilizing medication was the right thing to do in her case.

Patient 2

A 26 year old undergraduate female was self-referred for stimulant medication to treat Attention Deficit Hyperactivity Disorder (ADHD). She reported having a past history of ADHD since elementary school treated with methyphenidate as well as a past history of bipolar disorder treated with carbamazepine. She reported that her problems with mood resulted in multiple psychiatric hospitalizations in the past. However, at the time of presentation, she was on no psychotropic medication and was returning to school after a three-year absence.

The patient reported six psychiatric hospitalizations from age 13 through age 20. A review of hospital discharge summaries revealed a history of recurring depression characterized by a sad mood, lethargy, decreased appetite, irritability, and poor sleep interspersed with episodes of marked anger and aggressiveness both at home and school. Trials of antidepressant medication resulted in her feeling "hyper;" and she was observed having increasingly aggressive behavior and acting out, while taking antidepressant medication in the hospital. The discharge summaries stated that this picture seemed consistent with a hypomanic response to antidepressant medications. The diagnosis of bipolar disorder was made, and the patient was treated with carbamazepine 200 mg three times each day, and psychotherapy, with seemingly a good response. A telephone consultation with her mother revealed that when the patient was a child, methylphenidate helped her to focus in school, but seemed to contribute to mood instability. Her mother also reported that antidepressant medication made her happier than ever with limited sleep or more depressed and even (in her mother's words) psychotic. Her mother's report of her response to antidepressant medication and to stimulants was consistent with a bipolar subtype (type III) or bipolar spectrum disorder.

The discharge summaries also reflected a history of sexual abuse when she was four years old at the hands of an uncle, and physical and verbal abuse by her father until she was five years old and her parents divorced. She also had witnessed her father physically abusing her mother numerous times prior to their divorce. She had a fraternal twin sister who had a chronic medical condition requiring parental attention which left her feeling ignored and resentful. The hospital discharge summaries reflected a diagnosis of both bipolar disorder NOS and oppositional defiant disorder, severe type. During her public school years she was often truant from school. She would also fight with her sister and mother, and run away from home. When her confrontations with her mother and sister became violent, the police were called, and the psychiatric hospitalizations began occurring.

It was a combination of her clinical picture and her adverse response to antidepressant medications that prompted the diagnosis of bipolar disorder. She never fully followed through in her treatment. When she first started college, her friends would tell her that she had "an attitude problem" as she would often confront friends and co-workers and punch doors and walls. After completing the first two years of college, she took a leave from school to travel and live independently. She reported that she elected not to pursue any treatment for her mood swings because she felt this was something she wanted to accomplish on her own initiative without the use of psychotropic medication or the help of mental health professionals. By the time of her current presentation, she had returned to school to complete her last two years, and was financially independent and living on her own. She reported having one close friend and a full-time job. While there was some mild recurring depression, it was transient and not enough to interfere with her functioning. The chronic and recurring anger seemed to have subsided. She was more focused on becoming self sufficient though acknowledged sadly that it was difficult for her to find and maintain close friendships.

At the time of consultation, having been off all medication for over three years and free of any mood symptoms, she feared that being so distractible would interfere with the completion of her school work. She believed that she could take stimulant medications safely. As said, "I began to take charge of my life." She stated that over the past few years, she taught herself to refocus on something positive when earlier unwanted memories would come up. While she had acknowledged that in the past, she would feel more like an observer than a participant, most of the time, she now felt very much like a participant in her own life. She had one good friend, was steadily employed, and was active in a number of student affairs. She acknowledged with some sadness that her earlier traumatic history likely contributed to her tendency to push away intimate relationships, making her feel quite alone at times. During a college course on domestic violence, she became sad as she thought a lot about her father, but this was a brief depression lasting only a few days and was not accompanied by any acting out. She stated that her sister, who was ill with a chronic medical problem, was their parents' pet. She sadly recalled how difficult it was for her to get her parents' attention and had never been anyone's pet. Yet she did not want psychotherapy to address this problem.

While she did meet the criteria for attention deficit hyperactivity disorder, combined type, she no longer met the criteria for either bipolar disorder or for post traumatic stress disorder (or for conduct disorder). While I recommended that the safest treatment would be to start a mood stabilizing medication and then begin a stimulant medication, she insisted on being treated with a stimulant alone. She and her mother understood the risks of mood destabilization with such a treatment but agreed to accept the risk and to monitor her response closely. Amphetamine salts 10 mg twice each day was prescribed with good response in terms of substantially improving her ability to focus on her school work, and with no adverse affect on her mood over the course of one year of treatment.

Comment. This patient had at least one prior episode of major depression, at least one episode of observed antidepressant-induced hypomania, and recurring, brief, and early onset major depressive episodes. In addition, her mother observed her to have a hypomanic-like response to stimulants as a child. This picture was consistent with both bipolar III and bipolar spectrum disorder. She then had a good response to mood stabilizing medication. However, she took her treatment in her own hands after one year and stopped her mood stabilizing medication, making life changes that kept her away from being emotionally triggered and promoted new emotional connections and self-sufficiency. The picture of recurring depression and suicidal concerns disappeared. An independent and self-sufficient adult emerged who acknowledged taking responsibility for her behaviors. A trial of stimulant medication to help her complete her education made sense. A conversation that took place between the mother and the psychiatrist, when the patient was a child, confirmed both the benefit and the problem of earlier treatment with stimulants. So, treatment as an adult posed some risk. Stimulants are known to be destabilizing in patients with bipolar disorder who are not already taking mood stabilizers (Akiskal & Pinto, 1999). This patient was offered mood stabilizers before prescribing stimulants, but declined to take them. She was aware of the risks of taking stimulants, but her sense of herself being a different person as an adult proved correct.

Patient 3

A 28 year-old male, graduate student was referred by his psychotherapist for psychiatric evaluation due to periods of depression and hypomania. The patient described periods of more than four days at a time during which he would experience euphoria, decreased need for sleep with high energy the next day, flight of ideas, pressured speech, disorganized behavior, and impulsive spending. He also described other periods, lasting longer than two weeks at a time, of depressed mood, increased need for sleep, the wish to stay in bed all day, low energy, diminished concentration, feelings of hopelessness, and thoughts of suicide. The patient reported that sometimes there seemed to be a trigger for his episodes of depression or hypomania, but often they occurred for no apparent reason. There were more than four episodes per year beginning some time in his late teens. He reported that his brother was taking lithium and his mother had a similar mood pattern, but had not sought treatment.

His fiancé attended the next session and corroborated the patient's mood pattern. The symptoms of hypomania resulted in a depletion of his savings, and the patient's symptoms of depression prevented him from completing his schoolwork and regularly remaining employed. Both mood states interfered with his personal relationships. Based on the number and the duration of symptoms, as reported by the patient and corroborated by his fiancé; the adverse impact of the symptom on his life; and that the symptoms not being explained by neither a medical condition nor a substance abuse problem, the diagnosis of Bipolar I with Rapid Cycling was made (American Psychiatric Association, 1994), and divalproex was begun with good results.

He continued psychotherapy which addressed family issues–particularly his relationship with his mother who, as he reported, would in the past undo good things that happened to him. For example, she would take away his savings from a job to use it for family needs. The patient recalled that when he was in public school, he would come home from school hoping the "good mother," who was nice and kind, would be there that day rather than the "bad mother," who would criticize and hit him. He would always be puzzled about how his mother would hit him and his siblings repeatedly and then complain about them hurting her hand. He stated that because he was the one sibling who questioned their mother about her unpredictable behavior, he was made to feel like the black sheep of the family causing the family's problems.

With supportive psychotherapy and divalproex 500 mg at bedtime, there was an elimination of the hypomanic periods, but there were still some recurrent depression. For example, he called one day stating that he was feeling very depressed and anxious, and could not get out of bed for fear that if he left home, something awful would happen to him. Adding paroxetine 20 mg each day to the divalproex 500 mg at bedtime, and continuing psychotherapy around issues adjusting to being a student, resulted in his feeling euthymic.

After one year of doing well, he decided to stop all medications to see if he could get along without them. He did well for six months and then experienced another episode of depression. This time he required the combination of lithium carbonate 600 mg each day and divalproex 500 mg each day to achieve euthymia. Three months after feeling euthymic, he experienced a recurrence of depression with suicidal ideation, plan, and intent, requiring psychiatric hospitalization. At the time of hospitalization there was no evident precipitant save a recent separation from his fiancé, toward whom he described ambivalent feelings. His discharge medications included lithium carbonate, divalproex and venlafaxine.

During the subsequent partial hospitalization, he decided that he would take care of himself rather than take care of others. He felt that he was taking care of his fiancé without being cared for in reciprocal fashion. At that time, he recalled not only feeling emotionally abused by his mother but being sexually abused by a scout leader earlier in life. He also recalled being taken advantage of by a former employer. Then, the psychiatrist at the partial hospital stopped the lithium carbonate and divalproex, continuing only effexor 225 mg each day. His psychotherapy included both a bipolar support group and a men's group for survivors of sexual abuse. He continued in these groups for several months.

Soon thereafter, he became employed at a job that was of interest to him and gave him a chance to feel some mastery over problems he experienced in the past with people in authority. He discontinued group therapy and only came for medication management. He did well, save for periodic recurrences of depression that would come on over the course of a few days. When the depression peaked, he would stay in bed and be out of work for up to a week at a time. Then the depression would lift within a day without explanation. This was different from the prior pattern of mood instability, as there were no hypomanic episodes and the episodes of depression were shorter in duration. He began to see that he tried to do all his tasks at work perfectly, and would stay home from work (depressed and in bed) rather than do an adequate but less than perfect job. He negotiated a more reasonable work load with his demanding but understanding boss. Yet, the brief intermittent episodes of depression continued.

It was around this time that I had learned how to screen for dissociation. After one of the more recent episodes of brief depression, I asked him some questions about dissociative symptoms and he endorsed the following. Over the years, life had often seemed like a movie in which he was more of an observer than a participant. During the periods when he could not get out of bed, this depersonalization symptom was overwhelming and paralyzing. It turned out that he would experience the depressed mood, increased need for sleep, wish to stay in bed all day, low energy, decreased concentration, feelings of hopelessness, and thoughts of suicide, at the same time he was experiencing heightened symptoms of chronic depersonalization. At times such as these, he sometimes saw himself outside himself. He also described "feeling like a different person" when he was depressed and unable to get out of bed. He stated that when he was at work and feeling in a good mood, he could not recognize the person within him who stays at home and is afraid to leave the house. At this time, he agreed there was a connection between his symptoms of dissociation and depression and he agreed to a referral to a psychotherapist who had experience treating dissociative disorders.

No further formal evaluation of dissociation was pursued (to map out the extent of the dissociative diagnosis) because he felt quite engaged with his new therapist and was able to make considerable progress in psychotherapy. The venlafaxine was continued. During one subsequent episode of depression in which he missed over one week of work, he called to cancel an appointment. Both the patient and the psychotherapist asked about increasing the dose of venlafaxine. It was a mutual, three-way decision to keep the same dose. He was asked about upsetting thoughts or events preceding the latest episode of depression and none came to mind. Nonetheless the depression lifted after several days. He returned to work the next week.

During psychotherapy, he was able to identify triggering events in his current employment. When he understood what these triggers represented and how they prompted him to think about earlier traumatic experiences, his experience of heightened depersonalization and accompanying symptoms of depression diminished. He made some appropriate adjustments in his current work so as not to set himself up to feel victimized. Then his episodes of depression became fewer, shorter in duration, and less debilitating.

One year into this psychotherapy, he revealed that just before his hospitalization four years ago, a priest plied him with alcohol and forced him to have oral sex. This had not been reported at the time of the hospitalization as he had "forgotten" the experience until recently. The patient stated that the unwanted sexual experience with the priest reminded him of the unwanted sexual experience with a Boy Scout leader; and the experience was so overwhelming, at the time it occurred, that the patient "forgot" about it. The patient stated that he was feeling strong enough now to remember it.

As he was feeling more independent, he quit his full time job and has become self- employed, got married and began to complete his graduate education. To this day, nine years after beginning treatment for bipolar disorder, he continues in psychotherapy and the dose of venlafaxine (which has been his only psychotropic medication for the past five years) remains unchanged. He reports that he may get a day or two of a "brown out," but knows that he is being triggered somehow, thinks about it a bit, and pushes on. He no longer needs to stay in bed and avoid work.

There is a question in his mind, not yet resolved, as to whether or not the patient might slowly go off the venlafaxine some time in the future, once the recurrent episodes of depression and depersonalization stop, and he learns to yet better identify and manage his triggers. He did review this case report and the DSM-IV-TR, and said it made sense that the original picture looked like bipolar disorder. He also said that, in his opinion, the skills learned in psychotherapy (i.e., to identify current triggers being representations of earlier traumatic experiences and so not take the triggers too literally), permitted him to continue on with his life rather than become so reactive in either a hypomanic or depressed way. He could even see how some triggers (e.g., purchasing a new car and showing it to his mother who always envied people with nicer cars than she could afford) would make him feel euphoric. Other triggers (e.g., not being able to set limits with a very demanding supervisor at work) would make him feel depressed and victimized. The patient stated that he believed the intensity of his ups and downs gradually decreased over time with the help of psychotherapy, even though he has been without any mood stabilizing medications over the past few years.

After reading a draft of this article, the patient expressed an interest in completing a SCID-D in order to be sure there were no further unidentified dissociative symptoms, which he could address in psychotherapy.

While the patient is now married and self-employed, he states that his hesitancy in pursuing a full-time job, and therefore being employed by others, relates to his fear that he might again be triggered by someone in authority and not be able to report to work for a few days. He is hoping that further psychotherapy may help him gain confidence in this regard. A SCID-D-R revealed a longstanding and severe amnesia, severe depersonalization, mild derealization, significant identity confusion, with no clear identity alteration. This was consistent with the diagnosis of dissociative disorder not otherwise specified. As noted earlier in this case discussion, at times he would feel like a different person. Whether this was just related to being in a different mood or was, in fact, a different ego state, remains to be clarified. Clarifying issues such as this one or uncovering other possible dissociative symptoms should help him in his psychotherapy. There has been no reason to resume a mood stabilizer medication.

Comment. Patient 3 did have bipolar disorder I with rapid cycling as defined by DSM-IV. The assessment included an interview with his wife, who corroborated the diagnosis. Mood stabilizing medication was clearly warranted. While there was an awareness of earlier psychological trauma, there was no systematic assessment for dissociation early in the course of his treatment. Hence, the co-morbid dissociative disorder remained hidden for several years until I was trained on how to recognize and assess dissociative disorders. It was not until the patient described again recurring depressions (that were very brief but very debilitating), that I wondered if they could represent a dissociative phenomenon. It was then that I asked some questions about depersonalization. When depersonalization was endorsed as always present but much worse around the periods of brief depression, it became clear that his recurring depressions were dissociative in nature. This picture was there all along, I just did not have the diagnostic framework to properly assess it.

One might also ask whether or not his previous hypomanic episodes were dissociative in nature even though they met the DSM-IV criteria for bipolar disorder. Would he have had a good initial response to antidepressant medication? Would he have responded to psychotherapy that addressed his dissociative symptoms, and never needed any psychotropic medication? We will never know. He had matured considerably between the time mood stabilizers were started and the time they were stopped. That is, he became much more independent and less likely to involve himself with family conflicts. As a result, he was much less reactive to earlier traumatic experiences though he continued to have intermittent heightened depersonalization when triggered at times. I do not know why mood stabilizers were discontinued during his partial hospitalization, but I do know that the outcome was good.

Patient 4

A 25 year-old female presented with the chief complaint of severe premenstrual mood symptoms that interfered with her marital relationship and her ability to work. One dose of sertraline 25 mg made her hypomanic. The night after taking sertraline 25 mg, she reported having slept very little and having feeling euphoric. She described her experience as feeling like she was the center of the universe. She presented the next day with pressured speech and agitation. Further history revealed long-standing mood changes during her menstrual cycle, with the following sequence repeated each time: one week of euthymia in the middle of the cycle, followed by one week of murderous rage and irritability just before menstruation, followed by one week of mood swings during and shortly after menstruation, followed by one week of feeling very depressed. Over the years, the intensity of the symptoms increased. The patient described, when directly asked, intermittent olfactory hallucinations (either something burning or a musty smell), intense déjà vu lasting for hours and leaving her unable to do anything until it passed, and intermittent symptoms of depersonalization (e.g., seeing herself next to herself during stressful situations).

A neurologic work up yielded a normal neurologic exam, awake and sleep EEG, amd 72-hour ambulatory EEG. An abnormal MRI of the brain showed "a few non-specific T2 hyperintense foci" in the bilateral prefrontal subcortical white matter, which is found in some patients with bipolar disorder (Brambilla, Glahn, Balestrieri, & Soares, 2005). She had a normal CBC, liver functions, lipid panel, vitamin B-12, folate levels, ANA, RPR, homocysteine, methylmalonic acid, TSH, C-Reactive protein, and Lyme disease screen. Her history was consistent with Bipolar I with rapid cycling, including premenstrual and early postmenstrual exacerbation of her symptoms (American Psychiatric Association, 2000b). Based on her normal neurologic evaluation, it was felt that she did not have complex partial seizures. High doses of multiple medications were required to manage her agitation and sleeplessness (lamotrigine 200 mg twice each day, topiramate 100 mg twice each day, lithium carbonate 900 mg each day, bupropion 100 once each day, and clonazepam 1 mg at bedtime). Consultation with a bipolar specialist who had an interest in endocrine studies supported the diagnosis of "severe bipolar disorder with mixed symptoms, and premenstrual and early postmenstrual exacerbation of her symptoms." The recommendation was to add a "continuous" birth control pill to her treatment. She would take a birth control pill for seven weeks, and would have one week off. Three months into this treatment, the patient had some periods of euthymia and some periods of mild hypomania and mild depression.

Because the patient endorsed screening questions for depersonalization in the initial assessment, once her mood symptoms were no longer debilitating (so she could sit for an extended evaluation), a SCID-D-R was completed. This supported the diagnosis of Dissociative Disorder Not Other Specified (DDNOS). The SCID-D-R revealed a complicated inner life with its own private language of depersonalization, derealization, and identity confusion. Regarding amnesia, she reported hours to days missing beginning at around age 10, the longest time being about two weeks. It was while completing the SCID-D-R that she spontaneously reported how people "made fun of me constantly" for being overweight, beginning at around age 10. Regarding depersonalization, she described a spacey and floating feeling, as though her head would expand and get bigger or as though her arm moved even when still. She described these feelings as chronic, intermittent, and comforting. As a recent example, she went to a performance to keep a friend company, but wanted to leave the performance because the room was crowded and hot. She was able to stay in this physically uncomfortable environment by being comforted by the spacey and floating feeling she experienced through the entire concert. She also described feeling at times as though she was in a fog, isolated from the world. She reported that this long- standing and intermittent experience permitted her to function in her work at emotionally charged times.

When the patient began to read Kay Jamison's autobiography (Jamison, 1995), she noted how she experienced a sliding feeling, floating to the right and forward. Hence, she could not read the book. She reported that she was aware of feeling considerable anxiety over reading this book, and she could see how potential emotional triggers could cause her symptoms of depersonalization. Regarding derealization, she endorsed the previously-mentioned déjà vu. She described déjà vu as an intense feeling as though everything had happened before. The déjà vu was so intense that she had to stop what she was doing until it subsided. She would even go in to another room in hopes that a change of scenery would help it go away. This was chronic, recurring, and would last up to two hours at a time. Regarding identity confusion, she stated that since high school, "I never felt all there." Regarding associated feelings of identity disturbance in addition to the rapid cycling bipolar symptoms, she endorsed at times, "switching from angry to happy five times a day." These mood changes were associated with a rapid change in her ability to do her work and to get along with others. She also reported intermittent auditory hallucinations since age 10, characterized by either mumbling in the background or hearing a voice commanding her to do something. There was no identity alteration.

In retrospect, she believed that over many years she experienced either depression or hypomania, each lasting months at a time, until her more recent menstrual related mood cycling. This further corroborated the diagnosis of bipolar disorder. Her current diagnoses appeared to be Dissociative Disorder Not Otherwise Specified (DDNOS) as well as Bipolar Disorder I, rapid cycling. The patient agreed to continue mood-stabilizing medication and accepted a referral to a psychotherapist with an interest in treating dissociative disorders.

The initial goals of psychotherapy were to help her learn how to self-soothe at times of emotional stress, and to better identify and manage emotional triggers. Her current triggers included a supervisor who was threatening at times, and reminding her of her grammar school days when she experienced daily verbal insults regarding her obesity. In those days, she would stay in the ladies room where she would shake in the privacy of her stall. When the patient attended public school, she could only walk down the hall of school with a friend who would tell others to stop their taunting. She recalled that this went on day in and day out in her public school experience. She found that she preferred not to think about earlier childhood memories during therapy because in doing so she would "freak out." The patient reported that when she had recently opened her high school yearbook, she had to close it immediately as she felt very anxious and angry.

Her mood symptoms improved when she worked in psychotherapy on learning coping strategies to self-soothe in her present difficult work situation. The patient agreed that with each spike in symptoms, rather than consider changing her medication, she would look carefully at possible present and past triggers, and find ways to better manage them. Over time, there was a substantial improvement in mood stability and functioning. As the patient was better able to articulate her current life stressors and how they seemed to fuel her dissociative symptoms, her mood symptoms diminished and, in turn, the amount of medication required was cautiously cut back. One important focus of her treatment, which continually emerged, was whether new emergence of mood symptoms should be treated with medication change versus a psychotherapy intervention. This required careful communication between the prescriber, the psychotherapist, and the patient, to ensure there was a three way agreement regarding the approach to her treatment, at any one time. The question of life-long use of mood stabilizing medication is still up in the air; but over the first year of her treatment, there was gradual but substantial decrease in mood stabilizing medication. At the time the patient left the university, she was taking a birth control pill, diltiazem CD 120 mg each day, lamotrigine 600 mg per day, and escitalopram 10 mg per day. Diltiazem, a calcium channel blocker, was added to prevent migraine headaches (which began during the course of her treatment). Diltiazem also has mood stabilizing benefit, permitting her to cut back on other mood stabilizing medications. When she subsequently left the university and sought treatment elsewhere, she had been euthymic for several months.

Comment. This patient had a very complicated course in which her symptoms of bipolar disorder and dissociative disorder were intertwined. When an environmental trigger reminded her of earlier traumas, she would experience a transient heightening of her mood symptoms and dissociative symptoms, warranting a psychotherapy intervention and sometimes psychotropic medications. There had to be careful communication between the patient, her psychotherapist, and her prescriber to permit a consistent treatment approach.

Whether to address any change in her mood with psychotherapy alone or a combination of psychotherapy and medication adjustment resulted in a different answer each time. Further complicating her treatment was a changing bipolar picture over time. While she had a very clear picture of bipolar disorder in the past, characterized by weeks of depression or weeks of hypomania, more recently she experienced a rapid cycling picture coinciding with her menstrual cycle. This is consistent with Romans and Seeman's (2006) discussion in their section on bipolar disorder that "a subset of women may be reactive to the effects of cycling reproductive hormones" (p. 257).

Her long-term prognosis remains unclear. It is hard to know just how many years of treatment will be required before she feels that her dissociative disorder resolves. Even then, it will not at all be clear that it is safe to discontinue mood stabilizing medications. Whether or not her clinical course and MRI findings will be enough to warrant recommending life-long mood stabilizing medication remains to be seen.

Patient 5

A 69-year-old woman, who is now being treated for bipolar disorder and doing well on lithium carbonate 900 mg, lamotrigine 100 mg, risperidone 0.25 mg, and trazodone 50 mg each day, first presented for the treatment of winter depression at age 55 with no prior history of taking psychotropic medication. She had reported winter depressions for many years and finally decided to seek treatment.

The patient had noted that when traveling to the south during the winter, her depression would lift. A trial of bright light therapy produced good results; but the patient did not want to spend time sitting in front of the light each day. Hence, fluoxetine was started with good results, taken from early fall into early spring. During each spring and summer, she would do well without medication. It was noted that each year, she seemed to need a higher dose of fluoxetine to achieve euthymia, and that there was a several day period of heightened energy in the early spring, around the time she would taper off the fluoxetine. The diagnosis was changed from major depression, recurrent with seasonal pattern to bipolar II with seasonal pattern. A trial of lithium was started, but the patient stopped it due to side effects. She then dropped out of treatment for three years.

She returned to our clinic after being discharged from a psychiatric inpatient unit following what was termed a manic episode with psychotic features with onset during the fall season. The patient, however, believed that she was experiencing post traumatic stress disorder following childhood sexual abuse. She also believed that the hospitalization occurred because of her emotional reaction to the remembrance of earlier sexual trauma. She was discharged from the hospital taking lithium carbonate 450 mg, risperidone 0.5 mg and trazodone 50 mg each day. She stopped the medication soon after discharge from the hospital because she was convinced that she was experiencing post-traumatic stress disorder. Following a trip to the south, where it was warm and sunny, she became euthymic. Her only complaint remained her recurrent intrusive thoughts of being sexually abused at an early age.

She continued to believe that her own experience of manic-depressive-like symptoms had something to do with the emerging memory of earlier trauma and now that she was, in her words, coming to terms with this trauma, she was feeling better. She found psychotherapy around trauma-related issues and reading the book The Courage to Heal (Bass & Davis, 1988) quite helpful. The next fall, she became depressed and convinced her family physician to prescribe venlafaxine. When the patient met with me, she willingly added lithium carbonate and tapered off the venlafaxine. She did well through the next summer, taking lithium carbonate 600 mg each day (lithium level of 0.63 meq/L). When she became depressed the next fall, she refused a higher dose of lithium due to side effects; and so lamotrigine was added. The patient was concerned about the potential side effects of lamotrigine and so discontinued it. She requested adding fluoxetine to the lithium as this had helped her depression in the past. She became euthymic on this combination.

During the subsequent summer, her husband repeatedly called the clinic stating that she was noted to periodically lie on the floor in a fetal position, wailing about being sexually abused earlier in her life, spending money recklessly, being very argumentative, and staying awake long after her husband would go to bed. He was concerned that she was becoming manic. However, in the office setting, she stated that her mood was quite normal. She also appeared euthymic. The patient spoke with a normal speech cadence and response time. She reported that she liked time for herself after her husband went to bed. She also reported that what her husband considered reckless spending of money, she considered buying two kayaks an appropriate expense that they could both do together. The patient also indicated that she has been having emerging symptoms of post traumatic stress disorder for many years. First there was a recurrent image of a faceless person coming to mind. Then there was a sense of being triggered by reading the book The Courage to Heal. She was pursuing psychotherapy around recovering from memories of earlier sexual abuse.

A telephone consultation with her psychotherapist revealed that he had not observed any signs of mania or hypomania in the office. She also was reporting symptoms of pain in her feet, swollen ankles and elbows and feelings of malaise that were consistent with fibromyalgia. There was a question as to whether or not her symptoms of fibromyalgia and mood variability were a consequence of earlier emotional trauma. She experienced some trouble with her gait and so cut the dose of lithium back to 150 mg twice each day resulting in improvement in her gait. She continued to have what she described as flashbacks of earlier trauma and even began to believe she was beginning to see the facial features of the perpetrator. She was quite resentful that her husband did not support her through her reliving of her traumatic experience and resented that he interpreted her symptoms as being from bipolar disorder. She continued to see her psychotherapist twice weekly and seemed quite engaged in the trauma recovery process.

As she began to remember yet more information, she felt fearful even being in her own home and planned to spend a few days in a religious retreat. Her fear was so intense that at one point she called the police for protection. They brought her to the emergency room where she believed that she simply got carried away thinking about earlier trauma. She presented well dressed and well groomed. She spoke with normal speech cadence and response time. Her thoughts were coherent and goal-directed. There was no pressured speech, apparent flight of ideas, euphoria, or distractibility. While she initially seemed quite suspicious of others even in the emergency room, she settled down over the course of a few hours and seemed quite free of mood and psychotic symptoms. When offered psychiatric hospitalization, she refused. At that time, it was not felt that she met criteria for involuntary hospitalization.

She did agree to be driven to her favorite retreat and once there, to take a daily dose of an antipsychotic medication. This would address either the tremendous agitation of post traumatic stress disorder and/or mood disturbance that was part and parcel of bipolar disorder. After leaving the emergency room and traveling with others to her home, she elected to drive herself to the retreat. On the way there, she interpreted headlights from a car following her as someone who was going to hurt her. She sped upwards to 90 miles an hour to escape and crashed into a tree, totally destroying her car but leaving her with only a few bruises. She was taken to a local emergency room, where she was treated for bruises and released because the emergency room physicians did not see evidence of mania. Her family members caught up with her in the parking lot and brought her back to the hospital, where they convinced the hospital staff to admit her to the psychiatric unit. She subsequently had a 6 week inpatient psychiatric stay requiring risperidone 4 mg each day and lithium carbonate 900 mg each day to slowly achieve euthymia. Ultimately the dose of risperidone was decreased due to day-time sedation, and lamotrigine was added to treat a post-manic depression. The patient was finally discharged on lithium carbonate 900 mg, lamotrigine 100 mg, risperidone 0.5 mg, and trazodone 50 mg to be taken daily.

Over the next year and a half, her medications remained the same except for decreasing risperidone to 0.25 mg each day due to its sedating side effect. Currently she is euthymic and has no side effects from her medications. She no longer has any thoughts about earlier psychological trauma and is getting along well with her husband. Given her previous history of presenting one way to her mental health professionals and another way to her husband, he accompanies her to each visit. She reported feeling guilty about possibly transmitting the genes for bipolar disorder to her son, believing that this may account for why she was desperately trying to attribute her symptoms to something other than bipolar disorder. Whether or not her remembrance of earlier abuse is a mood-triggered occurrence or a fabrication to avoid the diagnosis of bipolar disorder remains unclear.

Comment. This patient had manic episodes with psychotic features in which denial of having bipolar disorder was part and parcel of the presentation (Yen, Chen, Yeh, [s6]Ker, Yang, & Yen, 2004). Furthermore, she had a first degree relative (her son) who had bipolar I and she desperately did not want to feel responsible for passing on bipolar genes to him. She managed to present herself to mental health professionals looking just fine but manifested her manic symptoms at home. As someone experienced working with survivors of physical and sexual abuse, she was able to incorporate her knowledge of abuse survivors into her own denial of her bipolar disorder. It is not clear whether or not she was a survivor of earlier abuse, the memory of which emerged when she was depressed. However, she should never stop mood stabilizing medication.

DISCUSSION

Patients 1, 2 and 3 met diagnostic criteria for both bipolar disorder and a trauma related disorder, benefited from mood stabilizing medications, and were able to successfully discontinue their mood stabilizing medication once their trauma related disorder improved. Patient 2 was ultimately able to safely take stimulant medication long after she experienced hypomania on antidepressants and on stimulants.

Does the transient nature of the bipolar disorder in patients 1, 2, and 3 mean that when mood symptoms consistent with DSM bipolar disorder or bipolar spectrum disorder are co-morbid with a trauma related disorder, it represents a subtype of bipolar disorder? Or, does this mean that bipolar-like mood symptoms are part and parcel of the neurobiology of trauma and it is a mistake to separate them in psychiatric nosology? It probably does not matter which way we look at it as long as the medication and psychotherapy provided are meeting the needs of the whole patient instead of addressing one part of the patient's suffering while ignoring the rest of the patient's experience. These cases have shaped my current approach to treating patients.

All of these patients taught me to evaluate patients for bipolar disorder they present with the picture of a trauma-related disorder, and to evaluate for a trauma-related disorder if patients present with the picture of bipolar disorder. These patients also taught me to think broadly about treatment. While I know that the psychotherapy recommendations for bipolar disorder include family focused treatment, interpersonal and social rhythm therapy, manualized CBT, psychoeducation, and Life Goals Program (Callahan & Bauer, 1999; Scott & Colom, 2005), I also know that I need to tailor the treatment to match the patient. Clemens (2005), in his article entitled "Flying High: The Myth of Specifity," discusses the importance of looking at the whole picture of patients with bipolar disorder and adjusting the intervention accordingly.

These patients also taught me to accept some uncertainty in the diagnostic process. There is some help in the literature with this point of view. Blacker and Tsuang (1992) stated that "no matter how we define criteria, considerable ambiguity about where and whether to draw lines between bipolar disorder and other disorders will remain" (p. 1476). They further state that "there are distinct limits to our ability to draw lines between disorders on the basis of phenomenology alone. At least for some psychiatric disorders, discrete categories may be an illusion." Blacker and Tsuang's article discussed these concerns by looking at the diagnostic boundaries of bipolar disorder. They stated:

> Personality disorders may simply mimic bipolar disorder, especially when they coexist with substance abuse . . . . They may also contribute to the development of bipolar disorder by unmasking latent symptoms. In addition, character disorders could in some cases result from developmental factors associated with growing up with bipolar disorder itself, with the liability to bipolar disorder, or with affected parents. Last, personality disorders may be modifiers of course, severity, or outcome. (p. 1478)

I would argue that the authors could have substituted the words trauma related disorders for personality disorders in the previous paragraph. The authors concluded their article as follows:

> At least for bipolar disorder, existing diagnostic criteria may represent the best that can be achieved by using current methods of case definition, but they may not be adequate for a number of research and clinical purposes. As information accumulates on other disorders and diagnostic criteria are refined, similar limits will be reached. If we are to continue our progress toward improved understanding and treatment of bipolar disorder and other psychiatric illnesses, we must begin now to develop the nosologic techniques of the coming century. (1481)

Because there is increasing recognition of the importance of formally assessing for trauma related disorders (Gold, 2004), Blacker and

Tsuang's recommendations should be taken very seriously. This article argues that future research in bipolar disorder should include careful screening for trauma related disorders.

Most research studies regarding bipolar disorder do not screen for disorders of psychological trauma. Because patients may present complaining of mood symptoms and their trauma related symptoms may be hidden, without adequate screening tools in the research protocol of a study, these patients will be missed. While PTSD is in the SCID-I and Borderline Personality Disorder is in the SCID-II, neither dissociative disorders nor complex PTSD are included in these diagnostic tools. Using diagnostic tools such as the Structured Clinical Interview for Dissociative Disorders or the Dissociative Disorders Interview Schedule helps to rule in or rule out a dissociative disorder. Using a diagnostic tool such as the Structured Interview for Disorders of Extreme Stress (SIDES–Pelcovitz, Van Der Kolk, Roth, Mandel, Kaplan, & Resick, 1997) or the Trauma Symptom Inventory (TSI–Briere, 1995 and Briere, Elliot, Harris, & Cotman, 1995) helps to rule out complex PTSD. Combining these tools with the PTSD component of the SCID-I and the borderline personality component of the SCID-II can help to rule out a trauma related disorder in patients who present with bipolar disorder. The combination of the SCID-I, PTSD section, SIDES, SCID-II Borderline Personality Disorder section, and the SCID-D in patients 6 and 7 are examples of how to complete such assessments in any patient who has bipolar disorder. If there is no trauma, testing may take less than one hour. If there is trauma, then it may take one to four hours. This is time well spent as it ensures that the patient's psychotherapy be tailored to addressing all of the relevant concerns.

Since the majority of studies of bipolar disorder do not use these screening tools in choosing their patients for long-term outcome studies, we do not know what percentage of patients in current bipolar studies have disorders of psychological trauma. Some patients with disorders of trauma may remain hidden; and this may be the explanation for patients with bipolar disorder having a chronic course, a severe course, or treatment refractoriness.

A recent study by Foote, Smolin, Kaplan, Legatt, and Lipschitz (2006) looked at the prevalence of dissociative disorders in psychiatric outpatients. A self-report measure of dissociation and trauma history was completed by 231 consecutive admissions to an inner city, hospital-based outpatient psychiatric clinic. All were offered an opportunity to complete the Dissociative Disorders Interview Schedule, and 82 accepted. A sample of 24 (29%) of the 82 interviewed patients received a diagnosis of a dissociative disorder whereas a chart review revealed only 4 (5%) had this disorder previously identified. These patients had a range of Axis I disorders including depressive, psychotic, anxiety and bipolar disorders. This study is an example of how trauma related disorders can be included in the screening assessments in a general practice setting with the result of completely changing how the patients are viewed diagnostically and completely changing the treatment recommendations. It would be very interesting to prospectively study a series of patients with bipolar disorder in such a fashion.

Sar and Ross (2006) discuss how dissociative disorders are a confounding factor in psychiatric research and have a number of suggestions on how to incorporate screening for dissociative disorders in bipolar disorders research. The same could be said for incorporating assessment devices for PTSD, borderline personality disorder, and complex PTSD, as well as for dissociative disorders.

When a disorder of psychological trauma is co-morbid with bipolar disorder, it does not matter whether the clinician sees two disorders or one disorder that has both mood and trauma features as long as the whole picture is addressed. Because some patients with both bipolar disorder and a trauma related disorder may complain about mood symptoms, but be willing to address the trauma related symptoms right away, the presence of these traumas needs to be kept in mind. Then, when the opportunity presents, appropriate psychotherapy needs to begin. Since some patients with bipolar disorder may not engage in a regular psychotherapy, this means that a prescriber needs to be alert to all the diagnostic possibilities throughout the treatment of any patient.

Screening patients for trauma disorders and using the term bipolar NOS for patients with co-morbid bipolar disorder and a disorder of psychological trauma is a way both to keep in mind the necessity of treatment beyond the current guidelines for bipolar disorder as well as keeping in mind the possibility of discontinuing the mood stabilizing medication once the disorder of psychological trauma significantly improves or resolves.

Patient five is a reminder of how vicious and hidden bipolar disorder can be and the respect clinicians must have when treating patients. However, unnecessary life-long mood stabilizing medication may exposes some patients to the considerable expense of medication and professional visits, side effects of medication and lack of satisfaction of healing from their disability. Hopefully future research will take into account the necessary screening tools so that we can better advise our patients on both their immediate treatment needs and their long-term needs to continue mood stabilizing medication.

CONCLUSION

The diagnosis of bipolar disorder using DSM-IV and bipolar spectrum criteria should not automatically mean that the patient needs life-long maintenance treatment with mood stabilizing medication. Naturalistic studies of bipolar disorder, completed before lithium, show that at least some patients have a self-limited course. This article suggests that at least some patients with a self-limited course have a co-morbid disorder of psychological trauma. Therefore, the identification and treatment of psychological trauma related disorders is essential when a patient has symptoms consistent with bipolar disorder. When this co-morbidity occurs, it is recommended that psychotherapy not only address the adaptation to experiencing bipolar disorder, but that it also be specific to the trauma related diagnosis. It is recommended that bipolar disorder be termed bipolar NOS when there is a co-morbid trauma related disorder in order to keep in mind the possibility of a limited course of treatment with mood stabilizing medications. It should be noted that many patients with bipolar disorder and disorders of psychological trauma have the need for life-long mood stabilizing medication and, for them, the risks of stopping mood stabilizers may result in treatment refractoriness and/or suicide. Prospective studies of bipolar disorder should reflect adequate screening for disorders of psychological trauma. Future research should try to clarify which patients need life-long maintenance medication to prevent treatment refractoriness and/or suicide and which can safely discontinue their medication.

REFERENCES

Akiskal, H. S. (2004). Demystifying borderline personality: Critique of the concept and unorthodox reflections on its natural kinship with the bipolar spectrum. *Acta Psychiatrica Scandinavica, 110*, 401-407.

Akiskal, H. S, Chen, S. E., & Davis, G. C. (1985). Borderline: an adjective in search of a noun, *Journal of Clinical Psychiatry, 46*, 41-48.

Akiskal, H. S., & Pinto, O. (1999). The evolving bipolar spectrum - Prototypes I, II, III, and IV. *The Psychiatric Clinics of North America, 22*, 517-534.

American Psychiatric Association. (1994). *Diagnostic and statistical manual of mental disorders (4th ed)*. Washington, DC: Author.

American Psychiatric Association. (2000a). *Diagnostic and statistical manual of mental disorders (4th ed., text revision)*. Washington, DC: Author.

American Psychiatric Association. (2000b). Practice guideline for the treatment of patients with major depressive disorder, second edition. *The American Journal of Psychiatry (supplement), 157*, 4-50.

Bass, E. & Davis, L. (1988). The Courage to Heal. New York: Harper & Row.

Benazzi, F. (2006). Borderline personality–bipolar spectrum relationship. *Progress in Neuro-Psychopharmacology & Biological Psychiatry, 30*, 68-74.

Blacker, D., & Tsuang, M.T. (1992). Contested boundaries of bipolar disorder and the limits of categorical diagnosis in psychiatry. *American Journal of Psychiatry, 149*, 1473-1483.

Brambilla, P., Glahn, D. C., Balestrieri, M., & Soares, J. C. (2005). Magnetic resonance findings in bipolar disorder. *Psychiatric Clinics of North America, 28*, 443-467.

Bolton, S., & Gunderson, J.G. (1996). Distinguishing borderline personality disorder from bipolar disorder: Differential diagnosis and implications. *American Journal of Psychiatry, 153*, 1202-1207.

Briere, J. (1995). *Truama symptom inventory (TSI) professional manual*. Odessa, FL: Psychological Assessment Resources.

Briere, J., Elliot, D., Harris, K., & Cotman, A. (1995). Trauma symptom inventory: Psychometrics and association with childhood and adult victimization in clinical samples. *Journal of Interpersonal Trauma, 10*, 387-401.

Callahan, A. M., & Bauer, M. S. (1999). Psychosocial interventions for bipolar disorder. *The Psychiatric Clinics of North America, 22*, 675-688.

Clemens, N. A. (2005). Flying high: The myth of specificity. *Journal of Psychiatric Practice, 11*, 123-125.

Foote, B., Smolin, Y., Kaplan, M., Legatt, M. E., & Lipschitz, D. (2006). Prevalence of dissociative disorders in psychiatric outpatients. *American Journal of Psychiatry, 163*, 623-629.

Ghaemi, S. N. (2003). *Mood disorders–A practical guide*. Philadelphia: Lippincott Williams & Wilkins.

Gold, S. N. (2004). The relevance of trauma to general clinical practice. *Psychotherapy, Theory, Research, Practice, Training, 41*, 363-373.

Henry, C., Mitropoulou, V., New, A. S., Koenigsberg, H. W., Silverman, J., & Siever, L. J. (2001). Affective instability and impulsivity in borderline personality and bipolar II disorders: similarities and differences, *Journal of Psychiatric Research, 35*, 307-312.

Jamison, K. R. (1999). *Night falls fast–Understanding suicide*, New York, N.Y: Alfred A. Knopf.

Levy, B. F., & Swanson, J. (submitted for publication, 2006) A qualitative study of the assessment procedures at a university mental health center specifically as they relate to the effective assessment of dissociative disorders. Manuscript submitted for publication.

Lucking, R. G. (1986). Bipolar disorder in post-traumatic stress disorder–a difficult diagnosis, case reports. *Military Medicine, 151*, 282-284.

Marangell, L. B., Silver, J. M., Goff, D.C., & Yudofsky, S. C. (2003). Psychopharmacology and electroconvulsive therapy. In Hales, R.C. & Yodofsky, S.C. (Eds.). *The American Psychiatric Publishing Textbook of Clinical Psychiatry,*

Fourth Edition (pp. 1047-1151). Washington, DC: American Psychiatric Publishing, Inc.

Paris, J. (2004). Borderline or bipolar? Distinguishing borderline personality disorder from bipolar spectrum disorders. *Harvard Review of Psychiatry, 12*, 140-145.

Pelcovitz, D., Van Der Kolk, B. A., Roth, S., Mandel, F. S., Kaplan, S., & Resick, P. A. (1997). Development of a criteria set and a structured interview for disorders of extreme stress (SIDES). *Journal of Traumatic Stress*, 10, 3-17.

Post, R. M. (2005). The impact of bipolar depression. *Journal of Clinical Psychiatry, 66 (suppl 5)*, 5-10.

Post, R. M., Leverich, G. S., Altshuler, L., & Mikalauskas, K. (1992). Lithium-discontinuation-induced refractoriness: Preliminary observations. *American Journal of Psychiatry, 149*, 1727-1729.

Post, R. M., Leverich, G. S., Xing, G., & Weiss, S. R .B. (2001). Developmental vulnerabilities to the onset and course of bipolar disorder. *Development and Psychopathology, 13*, 581-598.

Romans, S. E., & Seeman, M. V. (2006). *Women's mental health–A life-cycle approach*. Philadelphia: Lippincott Williams & Wilkins.

Ross, C. A. (1989). *Multiple personality disorder, diagnosis, clinical features, and treatment*, New York, N.Y.: John Wiley & Sons, Inc.

Sar, V., & Ross. C. (2006). Dissociative disorders as a confounding factor in psychiatric research. *Psychiatric Clinics of North America, 29*, 129-144.

Scott, J., & Colom, F. (2005). Psychosocial treatments for bipolar disorders. *Psychiatric Clinics of North America, 28*, 371-384.

Steinberg, M. (1995). *Handbook for the clinical assessment of dissociation, a clinical guide*. Washington, DC: American Psychiatric Press.

Yen, C. F., Chen, C. S, Yeh, M. L, Ker, J. H, Yang, S. J., & Yen, J. Y. (2004). Correlates of insight among patients with bipolar I disorder in remission. *Journal of Affective Disorders, 78*, 57-60.

doi:10.1300/J513v06n02_07

Trauma and Schizophrenia

Bertram P. Karon

SUMMARY. Schizophrenia is a chronic terror syndrome. In World War II there were battlefield traumas that always produced classic schizophrenic symptoms. However, if the patients were healthy before the trauma, they spontaneously recovered. The myth of the incurability of schizophrenia led to the belief that these individuals could not be schizophrenic if they recovered. But all schizophrenics are the victims of lives filled with trauma, sometimes subtle but usually obvious. Examples are described. Professionals have tried not to listen. But if one investigates, most of the bad things patients talk about or symbolize in their symptoms are not delusional, but real traumas. It helps to face the truth. doi:10.1300/J513v06n02_08 *[Article copies available for a fee from The Haworth Document Delivery Service: 1-800-HAWORTH. E-mail address: <docdelivery@haworthpress.com> Website: <http://www.HaworthPress.com> © 2007 by The Haworth Press, Inc. All rights reserved.]*

KEYWORDS. Trauma and schizophrenia, schizophrenia, trauma, psychotherapy of schizophrenia

Bertram P. Karon, AB, Harvard, MA, PhD, Princeton, is Professor of Psychology, Michigan State University, and Psychoanalyst, Michigan Psychoanalytic Council.

Please address correspondence to: Bertram P. Karon, PhD, Professor, Department of Psychology, Michigan State University, East Lansing, MI 48824 (E-mail: karon@msu.edu).

[Haworth co-indexing entry note]: "Trauma and Schizophrenia." Karon, Bertram P. Co-published simultaneously in *Journal of Psychological Trauma* (The Haworth Maltreatment & Trauma Press, an imprint of The Haworth Press) Vol. 6, No. 2/3, 2007, pp. 127-144; and: *Trauma and Serious Mental Illness* (ed: Steven N. Gold, and Jon D. Elhai) The Haworth Maltreatment & Trauma Press, an imprint of The Haworth Press 2007, pp. 127-144. Single or multiple copies of this article are available for a fee from The Haworth Document Delivery Service [1-800-HAWORTH, 9:00 a.m. - 5:00 p.m. (EST). E-mail address: docdelivery@haworthpress.com].

In World War II, every soldier who underwent a particular battlefield experience developed schizophrenic symptoms. The soldier was under fire. He was in danger of being killed. He dug a foxhole under fire as quickly as he could, one just barely big enough to get into. He crawled into it and stayed there. He did not eat or drink. He urinated and defecated on himself because there was no other place to urinate or defecate without being killed. If the situation lasted for several days, every single soldier appeared classically schizophrenic when the shooting stopped, and his buddies came up to him. That is, when these patients were finally rescued, they exhibited Bleuler's (1911) primary symptoms–thought disorder (inability to think logically when he wanted to), autism (inability to relate to other people), and apparently no affect or apparently inappropriate affect–plus hallucinations, delusions, and/or catatonic symptoms.

While these patients looked very severely schizophrenic, they recovered with safety and rest if they were reasonably healthy before this trauma. The term *schizophreniform psychosis* was invented to describe these patients, people who look in every way as if they are classic schizophrenic types, but who have a very good prognosis for spontaneous recovery (Bellak, 1948; Grinker & Spiegel, 1965). It was then believed that no schizophrenic patient ever recovered- a recurring myth in psychiatry–hence, a recovered patient must have been suffering from something else. Now we see these patients as simply one example of schizophrenic symptoms that occur in people who are reasonably healthy but subjected to unusual terror.

The true meaning of schizophrenia might have been discovered at that time if we had taken these observations seriously. Schizophrenia is primarily a chronic terror syndrome. Human beings are intended to be terrified for minutes, possibly for hours, so that emergencies can be dealt with. We are not intended to be terrified for days, weeks, or months. The only physiological findings with respect to persons with schizophrenia that can be replicated are those which are components of terror in non-schizophrenic individuals, or which are side effects of medications. The medications, which are helpful in the short run, are all medications which dampen down affect, including terror.

Eugen Bleuler's primary symptom of no affect is only apparently no affect, since terror masks weaker affects. All symptoms of schizophrenia are either manifestations of terror (e.g., not being able to think clearly, not being comfortable with people), defenses against terror (e.g., avoiding people, obsessive symptoms), or symbolic acts. Catatonic stupor is not a specifically human symptom, but the response of almost all animals as the last stage of defense when under attack by a predator (Ratner, Karon, VandenBos, & Denny, 1981), a stage in which they are conscious of everything that is going on, but do not flinch even when great pain is inflicted. The predator usually acts as if the prey is dead, and will leave it for later unless hungry, frequently saving the prey's life. This biological finding coincides with the clinical report by Fromm-Reichmann (1950) stating that catatonics know everything that is going on around them, even though they do not overtly react even to pain. The patients told her that when they were catatonic they had felt they would have died if they moved. As is so often the case, good laboratory research and good clinical observations coincide. There is, after all, only one real world.

The term *schizophreniform psychosis* was eventually abandoned, and then resurrected with an entirely different meaning in DSM-IV-TR (American Psychiatric Association, 2000) as schizophrenic symptoms that have lasted more than one month but less than six months. The myth of the incurability of schizophrenia, however, still echoes in DSM-IV-TR in the statement, "Complete remission (i.e., a return to full premorbid functioning) is probably not common in this disorder" (p. 309). This ignores the most important research findings on schizophrenia in the last 25 years: the 10 long-term, follow-up studies starting with Manfred Bleuler (1978), continuing with Luc Ciompi (1980), and the others from Switzerland, Scandinavia, Italy, Germany, and the United States (Harding, 1995; Harding, Zubin, & Strauss, 1987). Until Manfred Bleuler, no one had included patients who were not rehospitalized in studying the long-term course of schizophrenia. The general findings are that approximately a third of schizophrenics completely recover within 25 years irrespective of treatment, and this has been so since 1900. Another third of patients have social recoveries, that is, are able to function, work, and be self-sufficient, with some residual symptoms. Only approximately one-third has the classic morbid course still described in many textbooks.

Ciompi (1980) followed patients for 40 years in Switzerland. Ciompi reported that the "disease" of schizophrenia does not seem to follow the course of a physiological disease, but rather the order of the social crises in a human being's life experiences. No improvement has been shown in long-term outcome, with the introduction of modern medication, in any of the long-term studies. However, the best of the American long-term studies (Harding, 1988) found that 50% of schizophrenic patients stop taking their medication against medical advice, and the 30% who fully recovered in the long run were from that "non-compliant"

50%. No patient who continued to take their medication indefinitely as required by their psychiatrists had a full recovery, suggesting either that the healthier patients felt freer to stop against medical advice or that the medications, helpful in the short run, interfere with full recovery.

Every therapist who has ever listened to a person with schizophrenia has heard of a life filled with traumas. John Read and his colleagues (e.g., Read & Ross, 2003; Read, Goodman, Morrison, Ross, & Aderhold, 2005) have documented most carefully the frequency of histories of traumas in persons with schizophrenia as compared to both normal individuals and to patients with less severe diagnoses. This differential frequency is found even in the records of biologically oriented hospitals that make no effort to discover traumas.

These traumas have often been explained away either as delusional (i.e., as if the trauma never occurred), or as being the result of the illness (i.e., as if the patient arranges to be traumatized). Early in my career, when schizophrenic patients described traumatic events, particularly child abuse, I tended to consider them delusional until the evidence forced me to the conclusion that almost always the traumatic events had really occurred. In those few instances where the traumatic events are not real, they always represent a real problem that is distorted either in its recall or its description.

Evidence that the traumatic experiences were real was usually to be found in the recollections of members of the family, or sometimes in hospital records. In the 1950's and 1960's, families trusted mental health professionals to keep information confidential and to be concerned with helping their patients. Families were not as concerned as they are today about being reported for prosecution for having committed criminal acts or about being sued for damages. Of course, even then, most perpetrators lied. However, other members of the family did not often lie. In addition, some perpetrators told the truth because they regretted what they had done and hoped the mental health professional might be able to help the victim undo the bad effects.

Even harmful or abusive parents would often say, in private, that they were not proud of what they did, but that they had, in fact, done it. They might even say that they were ashamed of what they did while requesting us to help the child, "For God's sake, help the child." Although most of my patients have been adults, I have worked with a few schizophrenic children and have insisted that both parents be seen in therapy. I would see the child individually and then I would see each parent. Under those circumstances, it was easy to validate the reality of the bad events. (While I would still insist that both parents be in therapy, there are advantages and disadvantages to each of the alternatives: the same therapist working with child and parents, different therapists working with each person, or a family therapist working with the whole family in addition to individual sessions for the designated patient. In any case, someone must work with the parents if the child is to really get better.)

One eleven-year-old schizophrenic boy reported an anxiety dream: "I was looking at a picture of a machine consisting of a needle and a bowl. Then an ape was chasing me. And I woke up." In his next session, the father stated that when the patient was small, his crib was in the parents' room.

"But he used to stand up and look at us."

"Was it annoying?"

"It sure was. He used to make noise.

"Did you hit him?"

The father hesitated and then stated that he used to hit his son and felt guilty about it. "Was that when you were having sex?" The father was startled at the question, but then said that in fact he felt guilty when he hit the child because it was embarrassing. The father stated that it had happened many times and he was ashamed of it now.

An 18-year-old freshman woman from a small town left home for the first time to go to a small Catholic college at some distance from her home. She had a psychotic break apparently for no reason. Her family thought that leaving home seemed to have been too stressful for her. When she was hospitalized, the treating psychiatrist described her as a "totally uncommunicative patient," and consequently recommended a course of electro-convulsive therapy (ECT).

On my recommendation, her parents withdrew permission for ECT, arranged for testing with a competent clinical psychologist, and a consultation with me. By the time of the consultation (three days later), her psychiatrist rethought his recommendation and told the patient and her parents that he now thought that ECT would be a mistake.

The psychologist (Mary Jane Keller) was able to relate to the patient so well that the patient took the tests without any problem, on the same day that she was to be interviewed by me. Dr. Keller relayed her findings to me over the phone, before I talked the patient. On the basis of the kindly relationship formed with the diagnostic psychologist during the testing, it was much easier to relate to the patient. I let the patient know I wanted to help. I told her who I was, what I knew about what was going on, what had happened, and that she had been saved from the trauma of ECT by my recommendation, which even her psychiatrist now admitted would have been a mistake. I said I wanted to see what else I could do that might be helpful. (Since I was scheduled to go on sabbatical at the end of the term, I had only agreed to see her and make a recommendation.) I wanted to hear what had happened, and I took seriously what she told me. By the end of the hour she was talking freely, and it was clear to me that even in ten weeks we could get a lot of work done. We began psychotherapy with the understanding that we would interrupt therapy at that time.

The Thematic Apperception Test indicated a trauma that had precipitated the psychosis. This was confirmed by the patient. At college, she had met a boy and gone out with him. But he wanted sex and she did not. One evening, they were walking alone nearly a mile away from any building (the small college was in a rural area). The boy became frustrated and told her that he was going to rape her. This terrified her.

Given their isolation, it would have been impossible for her to stop him. He did not rape her, so obviously he had no intention of actually raping her but of scaring her into compliance. But she believed he was going to rape her, and she was terrified. That was the precipitating trauma, and she fell apart. Interestingly enough, he had also dropped out of college. She never did find out anything about his later life. She tried to see a psychologist at the College who recommended that she return home. The patient saw a psychiatrist, who medicated her. This did not help, and the patient was hospitalized.

But she did respond to psychotherapy, without medication, with a therapist who listened. She was out of the hospital after 3 sessions, started living on her own, earned her living doing housework while she continued psychotherapy twice per week, and ended therapy as planned at the end of 10 weeks. At that time, she was making arrangements to return to college. She also knew that she could ask for and receive more psychotherapy at our University clinic if she asked for it, even if I was not there. She started college, ran into difficulty, and returned asking for therapy. She was seen in psychoanalytic therapy for a year by a graduate student under supervision. She dropped out college, took a brief secretarial course, started earning a better living, and got married. After a few years she returned to college to finish her education while her husband finished graduate school.

However, there were also longer lasting subtler traumas. It is my practice to allow immediate family members one confidential session. Her mother said in that confidential session that she had never been able to love the patient. There were many children in this family. Her mother said this was the only child she had never been able to love. The mother felt guilty about it. She had never told the patient this. But she was honest with me because she was afraid that it had something to do with her daughter's problems. Indeed, that daughter was the only child in the family who ever had a psychotic break. Her mother's honesty and concern made it easier for me to understand the patient's feelings. (Of course, I never told the patient what her mother said, but it was easier to give credence to the patient's feelings of not being loved. If I felt it was necessary to tell the patient, I would, of course, have gotten her mother's permission first.)

A 32-year-old paranoid schizophrenic patient in his thirties had been hospitalized as psychotic for 16 years (Karon & Rosberg, 1981). He spent only half of those years in mental hospitals. He was never discharged, but he was a genius at escaping. His mother sent him money to live on until he got into difficulty and was rehospitalized. I treated him for a year in a residential treatment center, five sessions per week without medication. This was followed by a second year of treatment under Jack Rosberg, a colleague, and several years of outpatient therapy. Thirty years later he has lived a successful life with no relapses.

When he started treatment with me, he insisted, "my mother was nice, my father was nice, my family was nice, and nothing happened in my childhood." According to both him and his mother, the precipitating event was the death of his father. When the patient was 12 years old, his father died from what may have been an accident. Certain circumstances, however, strongly pointed to the possibility of suicide. But his mother never told him how his father died "to spare his feelings." (Of course, the fantasies generated by keeping things mysterious are usually more traumatic than any unpleasant event, but his mother did not know that.) His mother described the family situation before the death of his father and, in fact during his whole childhood as "happy." After his father's death, the boy began to hear the voices of drowned people when riding a car by a river or a lake. He developed a strong interest in spiritualism and heard the spiritual world, that is, dead people talking to him.

With these hallucinations, which obviously had the reassuring meaning that death was not real, that it did not matter if you were alive or dead, he was able to function in school and other situations for years. During this period, his mother took him to a Park Avenue psychiatrist to have the psychiatrist talk to him about sex. During the interview, the patient was continuously hallucinating, but at the end of the interview the psychiatrist told the patient's mother that the patient was the best adjusted teenager he had ever seen. According to the patient, "You just tell a psychiatrist you know nothing about sex, and they say you are well adjusted."

Eventually, he complained about a conspiracy against him in which his mother was involved. He was then hospitalized, and began his career as a patient. During his latest treatment his mother, supposedly to save money, started living with him in the residential treatment house where he was treated, helping to take care of it. Their informal interactions were thus observable during this time. His mother had been psychoanalyzed. She consciously tried to be helpful, but was actually destructive, by insistently repeating to the patient the more or less classical interpretation of death wishes towards his father. In fact, there was nothing in the patient's behavior or conversation outside the therapeutic hour which seemed related to such feelings. Nor was there any material in the therapy hours related to such feelings.

Literally hundreds of times with no provocation, the mother asked the patient, "Do you think you killed your father? You didn't kill your father. Nobody blames you for killing your father." Eventually, the patient revealed that 6 months before the death of his father, his mother had left, saying she wanted a divorce and later returned "because she needed money." Eventually, the patient was able to recall the "civil war" he felt inside him when having to choose between his mother and father, he chose his father.

The father had been a weak ineffectual character, nevertheless loving as compared to his mother, and hence a sustaining force in the patient's life. The patient recalled having had his first hallucination when he learned that his father was dying. He prayed to God to save his father's life, and a voice told him that his father would be spared. The next day, his father died. The patient felt that his mother had killed his father and would kill him too if he ever got her mad.

There were anal problems. His mother described him as having been completely toilet trained before the end of the first year, which can only be done traumatically. Just how strong the resultant fears of his own feces were in this patient was shown in the fact that he would periodically fast insofar as the therapists and attendants would allow it, even after his fears of being poisoned (which will be discussed below) were resolved. These fasts were not terminated until the patient was explained that if he could stop eating he would "not have to shit." The therapist actually accompanied the psychotic patient to the bathroom when he defecated and continued talking with him to indicate that his feces were not repulsive, discussing later in therapy the meanings of toilet training and feces.

The importance of these anal pressures to the patient was shown when he was asked in a therapy hour to talk about the envy he felt for his younger brother. He immediately said:

"There is no envy about shit."

"Do you remember anything about shit?"

"My brother shit in the bathtub when he was five years old and my mother cleaned it up."

"If you had shit in the bathtub at that age, what would have happened?"

"I don't know."

"Would your mother clean it up?"

"No."

"Would you be punished?"

"Yes."

"How would they have punished you?"

"I don't know. But it would be awful."

We see that the patient's feeling about his brother being more loved than him was, in fact, based on preferential treatment. Moreover, when his brother was born, the patient, who was four years old, suffered from whooping cough, and was tended by his mother personally while he was confined to bed. Suddenly, his mother left him to have the second child and did not come near him for almost two months, a minor eternity to a sick 4-year old. No wonder he felt that his mother loved his younger brother more.

The patient talked about oral problems (Karon, 1960) including the fear of being poisoned, which sometimes caused him not to eat. Nonetheless, his mother, who consciously wanted to be helpful, was proud of the fact that she had breast-fed the patient for a full year, and had gradually weaned him. Where, then, could there have been an oral trauma?

During the early weeks of therapy, the patient refused to drink milk. He finally told the therapist, "The Athenian girls are laughing at me. They say their breasts are poisoned." The therapist reassured the patient that the therapist was stronger than the Athenian girls and that the milk was not poisoned. The patient then asked for and received a large glass of milk which he drank, asked for another glass which he also drank, and showed no specific distaste for milk afterwards.

One day while sitting down, the patient was approached by a woman with a rather well endowed bosom. He made frantic wiping gestures from his side. Afterwards, he told the therapist, "She approached me with her breast and I got hurt in the side." One day while sitting at breakfast, the patient's mother, who was knowledgeable about psychoanalysis, asked him, "Didn't I have enough milk? Didn't I give you enough to drink?" The patient replied, "The cow gave her calf milk and then kicked it. She shouldn't do that. It's something that happened hundreds of times in the history of the world." During therapy, the therapist reminded the patient of this statement. The patient steadfastly denied that the statement had anything to do with him, "It's just something that happened. The cow gave her calf milk and kicked him. It has nothing to do with me." The milk or food seemed to be poisoned not by any characteristic of the milk but by the fact that his mother had resented any demands upon her to feed the infant, so that after feeding him, she would become immediately angry. Then, the child would feel her hostility and get hurt. To an infant, an angry mother is a trauma. The trauma did not happen once but over and over. This problem continued even after the patient became an adult. Whenever the patient's mother cooked a meal and he ate it, there was a quarrel afterwards. If the patient did not eat (sometimes he was on a fast or hunger strike) or if the mother did not cook (often the attendants cooked), there was no quarrel. The attendants reported that the problem went on, in this sequence and without exception, for six months. The quarrel would be neither about cooking nor about food, but about something different each time. Apparently, the demand to feed made the mother angry; and when she became angry, anything would turn into a quarrel. The mother was not consciously aware of this sequence. The patient would also deny, even during therapy hours, being consciously aware of this, although his delusion of the cow clearly reflected it, and our discussion on the meaning of that delusion led to the disappearance of his fear of being poisoned.

Patients often resist the idea that their parents were involved in a trauma or that they were not above reproach. Once, a patient told me how lucky he was to have had such good parents, especially such a good mother. However, even before becoming psychotic, the patient had not been able to remember anything about his life prior to the middle of high school. The patient had not thought this abnormal. After unsuccessful "psychotherapy," combined with multiple medications in increased dosages, and inpatient treatment, all of the patient's psychiatrists diagnosed him with an "incurable schizophrenia." Electro-convulsive therapy (ECT) was recommended as his only hope. His wife was told that although ECT would probably not help, it was his only hope.

On my advice, his wife withdrew permission for ECT and removed him from the hospital. At that point, the patient was not eating or sleeping, and was continuously hallucinating. He was seen in psychoanalytic therapy, without medication, seven days on the first week, six days on the second week, and five days on the third week. He was very gradually reduced to four times per week, and then to three. After the third year, the patient was seen on a once-per-week basis. The patient began eating after three days, began working at a complex job after six months, and eventually had a successful and creative career while becoming a good husband and father.

In one of his hallucinations, the client would feel the horrible experience of burning in Hell. A friend of the couple, who had suggested to the wife to talk to me and had asked me whether the patient might be treatable, asked me early in the treatment whether the patient had ever talked about the scar on his hand, suggesting that I ask the patient about it. When I asked the patient whether he had a scar on his hand, he told me that he did. The patient's mother told me the story behind the scar. According to her, she took the patient to a store when he was five years old. Seeing him with a toy in his hand, the mother asked him where he had gotten it. He said that a lady had given it to him. The mother asked the lady, who stated that she had not given him the toy. The mother made him return the toy and apologize to the lady. Then, she took him by the hand, walked him home four or five blocks, took him up the stairs to the third floor where their apartment was, turned on a gas burner, and held his hand in the burner to teach him not to steal. Although the burn left a permanent scar, the patient sustained that the event had no effect on him because he could not remember it. I told the patient that I was of the opinion that what we cannot remember has the most profound effect on us. I added, "Most of us can only imagine what it would be like to burn in Hell. But you've actually been there." His hallucination of burning in Hell disappeared after that session.

Another trauma that he recalled included being sent out to play dressed all in white when he was five years old, and receiving a beating if he got dirty, which of course, he did. The patient deemed this punishment appropriate. I pointed out to the patient that any parent knows that a child of that age, dressed all in white, would get dirty within 30 minutes even in a hermetically sealed room.

The patient grew up in an Italian neighborhood in New York City. As he would go out to play, his mother would warn him not to play with Italian kids, "for his own good" because "those Italian kids" were dangerous. Of course, in an Italian neighborhood in New York City, there are only Italian kids. Hence, he would have to either not make friend or do wrong (according to his mother's dictates) by the friends he made.

The patient had always tried to be good enough to deserve his parents' love. As a child, the patient together with his brother would receive piano lessons. The patient worked hard to develop some skill. His brother apparently had little talent, so the piano teacher gave up and taught the brother a couple of pop tunes. The patient eventually became ready to show off to his parents the skill with which he had learned to play after considerable effort. But when he played the piano for them, the patient discovered that the parents did not like his classical music but enjoyed his brother's pop tunes.

The patient had the fantasy that if only he were successful enough, his parents would eventually love him. However, whenever his parents talked to him on the phone or in person, they would only talk about how much money his brother (who had gone into business) was making. Similarly, when they talked to the brother, they would only talk about how brilliant the patient was. Both brothers felt like a failure before psychoanalytic therapy, which they both luckily undertook. I pointed out to the patient that both he and his brother were successful and that there is not enough time in life to do everything. If you are a college professor, you are not going to earn a great deal of money. If you are a businessman, you are not going to write books. His parents were neither intellectuals nor successful business people, but they were good at making both of their children feel inadequate despite their success. When the patient finally finished his PhD, he was given a raise and a promotion in his academic job. He called his parents to share his triumph and get the approval he now felt he had earned. His parents did not react, except to ask whether that was all the salary he got. "I've been telling people you make more than that already," said his father. After that phone call, the patient's defenses began to unravel, and he got sicker and sicker until his hospitalization.

The patient's mother had produced in him the feeling that food outside the family was dangerous. The patient's wife reported that when they ate out, the patient would regularly ask, "Is it safe to eat this?" The patient reported that he had never eaten a meal without feeling nauseated. When we started psychotherapy, we focused on the fact that the patient was not eating at all, given that this symptom could become fatal in 30 days. I took him early in the morning to an all-night restaurant. He objected, "I can't go in there. They'll think I'm crazy." I told him that, on the contrary, they would think he was drunk. "I'll throw up!" I told him that he would not be the first drunk to throw up there that night. As I have recommended for patients who do not eat (Karon & VandenBos, 1981), I ate one meal a day with him, in this case, breakfast, and we talked about eating. Most important with psychotic patients who do not eat is the fear of being poisoned, which usually relates to the repetitive trauma in infancy and childhood of a mother who resents (usually unconsciously) having to feed and mother the child, consequently getting angry after each time she feeds the child and the child eats. As discussed before, neither the mother nor the child is usually aware of this. Our discussion of such a possibility in his family led him first to get angry at me. He took a cup of black coffee on our second restaurant session, coffee and toast on the third, and then began to have breakfast and eat regular meals. Years later, when he visited Paris, he recounted with tears in his eyes, "I can't tell you what French cooking is like. There is nothing like it in America." I knew I had helped him.

Six months after beginning intensive psychoanalytic therapy without medication, this "incurable schizophrenic" was back at work on a full-time basis as an academic. The patient stayed in treatment for years, working on new issues including his difficulty about writing his first book, his experience of psychosomatic problems, his marital problems, and his need for help in undoing the harm he felt he had done to his now adolescent son, who had a psychotic father when he was young. The patient stated, "that was a hell of a thing to do to a kid and I need help in undoing the harm I did him."

The patient ended up becoming a good father and husband, an excellent teacher, and a first rate scholar with an international reputation. He sent me a note about a prestigious award he received stating that he had never really expressed his thanks to me for returning a life to him. (I felt that he had appropriately thanked me, but he apparently did not.) Remembering the trauma of never having his excellence appreciated by his parents, I wrote him a note saying, "From time to time I have heard from students about your teaching and from colleagues in your field about the importance of your contributions, and it has always been a source of satisfaction that I was available when you needed me."

One year, I taught a seminar about Psychotherapy of Psychosis for residents in psychiatry at a state hospital. I clearly made them anxious because I sustained that lobotomy (which was still being done) was destructive, that Electro-Convulsive Therapy (ECT) was destructive, that medication was of limited benefit, and that residents should be talking to and listening to their patients. That was not what their other supervisors had said even though the Director of resident training had asked me to teach the seminar to the residents. Indeed, at first, members of the psychiatric staff attended the seminar. However, the residents asked that the psychiatric staff be excluded. They told the director of resident training that the staff made so many objections that the residents felt they were not being allowed to learn. The residents said they already knew what the staff thought and wanted to hear, at least, what I had to say. Nonetheless, I made them anxious. They asked me to interview a patient. Most schizophrenics are not dangerous. However, the residents showed their hostility by choosing a patient who was very muscular, moved very fast, and had a history of assaulting strange men. Knowing that they had never been that close to anyone that dangerous, who moved that fast, I got even by insisting that they sit in the same room with us during the interview. At least I knew some things about violent people that I could rely on while they did not, and that if I found him scary, they would be ten times more scared. The patient was not only dangerous, but also grossly incoherent. Whenever he was not incoherent, he stuttered very badly. The only way the residents could have found a patient seemingly less suited to verbal psychotherapy would have been finding a patient who either could not talk at all or only talked a foreign language.

There were over ten years of hospital records on him, the length of time he had been a patient on the locked chronic ward. In those records, which included a family history, there were apparently no traumas that would account for the severity of his problems. He grew up in a lower socioeconomic family in Detroit. His father was an alcoholic. He had developed a speech disorder (stutter), which did not respond to speech therapy. Eventually he went into the army. He showed up on sick call with a venereal disease, the site of infection being his mouth. Shortly thereafter, he assaulted a stranger supposedly for no reason, but never received a general discharge. His history then became to be hospitalized as severely disorganized, pull slowly together, be discharged and soon assault another stranger, and be rehospitalized as a disorganized schizophrenic.

The traumas came to light in therapy. He had a symptom that worried the attendants: From time to time, he would grab a patient and choke him until the victim, feet in the air, would become unconscious. The patient had not killed anyone yet, but the attendants were concerned that he might. In my value system, which most patients share, the first issue to deal with is possible homicidal danger, followed by possible suicidal danger, followed by anything else. Consequently, I continually brought up this symptom in the first session. Despite the patient's apparently incoherent remarks, he was able, bit by bit, to tell me how his mother would put a cloth around his neck and would choke him for minor offenses such as not eating. Since all of us biologically go into panic when our ability to breathe is suddenly cut off, the repeated early childhood trauma must have been unbearable for him. After he and I had reconstructed and discussed this trauma, his choking other patients ceased permanently.

Although we do not always get a dramatic immediate improvement even when we are right, it is a useful rule of thumb to assume that we are doing the right thing when we do get a dramatic improvement in a long-lasting symptom. The meaning of the symptom was his undoing the trauma. He would re-enact the trauma by playing the role of his mother while the victim played the role of the patient. The patient was proving that the mother would have never killed him because he would stop the choking when the victim was unconscious but still alive. The symptomatic act reduced anxiety, but would have to be repeated eventually. It was only when the patient consciously linked the symptom, the trauma as actually experienced, with its meaning, that he understood the symptom and as well as the fact that his mother would never choke him again. The symptom was resolved.

A second trauma came to light in a transference reaction. Once, the patient began a session by shouting at me, "Why did you do it to me, Dad?" Some organically oriented mental health professionals might have simply noted that the patient was obviously confused. But it is not hard to recognize a transference reaction when the patient calls you, "dad," or "mom." I asked the patient what I had done, but he would only shout angrily, "You know what you did!" I asked him how old he was; and he said that I knew he was eight years old. Bit by bit, the patient told me that when he was eight years old, I came home drunk and anally raped him. Of course, there were more bad things in his life besides these isolated traumas. One might as well ask what type of mother would choke her young child, what type of father would rape his eight year old son under any circumstances, and what type of life the client would have led with his family.

Anna Freud, in the Harvard lectures of 1948, compared the reconstructions of psychoanalyses of young adults with the events that had actually happened in their childhood while growing up in the Hampstead Clinic, where the events were recorded (Freud, 1992). If the psychoanalyses were at all careful, the reconstructions were accurate, with one exception. What was remembered or reconstructed as a single event in the psychoanalysis always represented a series of events with a similar meaning. Memory seems to consist of summaries. This is consistent with Sigmund Freud's statement that all of childhood is contained in the "screen" memories, that is, the apparently isolated and often seemingly meaningless memories of childhood, which when explored and associated to, lead to the important issues and events of childhood, even those repressed (unavailable to conscious recall).

The obvious traumas in this patient's life involved more than his parents. When he was not grossly incoherent, he stuttered very badly. His stutter had an unusual basis. In the middle of his confusing utterances, I would suddenly hear words in Latin. (In high school they told me that if I wanted to go to college, I should take Latin. I took four years of Latin, and at this one time of my professional career, it became useful). It took me several minutes to wonder how this uneducated man had learned Latin before I thought of altar boys. I asked the patient whether he had been an altar boy. He stated, "You swallow a snake and then you stutter. You mustn't let anyone know." The patient seemed very ashamed and guilty. I took the symbolism seriously and guessed that he had probably performed fellatio. He seemed too guilty for it having involved another altar boy. I interpreted it as a sexual experience, an oral one, because with schizophrenic patients much of what seems sexual is really related to morality and survival. In addition, while a snake may represent a penis (because of its shape, extensibility, and dangerousness), a penis may also represent a breast, and a breast may represent love. I told the patient, "I know what you did with the priest, and it's all right. Anyone as hungry as you were would have done the same thing." His stuttering, which had lasted many years and which had resisted the efforts of a speech therapist in high school, immediately stopped. When the stuttering resurfaced in subsequent sessions, it became possible to stop it immediately by repeating the same interpretation. For many years, when I mentioned this case at professional presentations, there would always be someone who objected that I had no evidence that the patient had actually been molested by a priest, and that, after all, a priest would not do a thing like that. In recent years no one makes that objection.

This patient, whose severe schizophrenic symptoms seemed so puzzling in terms of the many years of recorded professional notes documenting treatment by practitioners who medicated without listening, now made good sense. His mother was horrible. When our mother is bad or defective, we turn to our father. But the patient's father was horrible. Finally, the patient turned to God; and even the priest was horrible. Wouldn't that drive any of us crazy?

In my view, most psychopathology is the result of trauma. The question is not whether or not there were traumas, but what were the traumas, what was the nature of those traumas, what effects they had, and what we need to do to help. People suffering the most serious of emotional problems, those we call schizophrenic, have simply had the most devastating traumas. We can discover what these traumas were and what needs to be done, if we are willing to hear, listen, and help.

REFERENCES

American Psychiatric Association (2000). *Diagnostic and statistical manual of mental disorders (4th ed.), text revision.* Washington, DC: American Psychiatric Association Press,

Bellak, L. (1948). *Dementia praecox.* New York: Grune & Stratton.

Bleuler, E. (1911). Dementia praecox or the group of the schizophrenias. In J. Zinkin (Trans.). *The schizophrenic disorders: Long term patient and family studies.* New Haven and London: Yale University Press.

Bleuler, M. (1978). *The schizophrenic disorders: Long term patient and family studies.* New Haven and London: Yale University Press.

Ciompi, L. (1980). Catamnesic long -term study on the course of life and aging of schizophrenics. *Schizophrenia Bulletin, 6,* 606-617.

Freud, A. (1992). *The Harvard Lectures.* In J. Sandler (Ed.), New York: International Universities Press Inc. (original work published 1952).

Fromm-Reichmann, F. (1950). *Principles of intensive psychotherapy.* Chicago: University of Chicago Press.

Grinker, K. R., & Spiegel, J. P. (1965). *Men under stress.* New York: McGraw-Hill.

Harding, C. M. (1988, July). *Chronicity in schizophrenia.* Paper presented at the International Association of Psychosocial Rehabilitation Services conference, Philadelphia, PA.

Harding, C, M. (1995). The interaction of biopsychosocial factors, time, and course of schizophrenia. In C. L. Shriqui & H. A. Nasrallah (Eds.), *Contemporary issues in the treatment of schizophrenia* (pp. 653-681). Washington, DC: American Psychiatric Press.

Harding, C.M., Zubin, J., & Strauss, J. S. (1987). Chronicity in schizophrenia: Fact, partial fact, or artifact? *Hospital and Community Psychiatry, 38,* 477-486.

Karon, B. P. (1960). A clinical note on the significance of an "oral" trauma. *Journal of Abnormal and Social Psychology, 61,* 480-481.

Karon, B. P., & Rosberg, J. (1981). The mother-child relationship in a case of paranoid schizophrenia. In B. P. Karon., & G. R. VandenBos (Eds.), *Psychotherapy of schizophrenia: The treatment of choice* (pp. 337-353). New York: Jason Aronson.

Karon, B. P., & VandenBos, G. R. (1981). Psychotherapy of schizophrenia: The treatment of choice. New York: Jason Aronson.Ratner,

Ratner, S. G., Karon, B. P., VandenBos, G. R., & Denny, M. R, (1981). The adaptive significance of the catatonic stupor in humans and animals from an evolutionary perspective. *Academic Psychology Bulletin, 3,* 273-279.

Read, J., Goodman, L., Morrison, A. P., Ross, C. A., & Anderhold, V. (2004). Childhood trauma, loss, and stress. In J. Read, L. R. Mosher, & R. P. Bentall (Eds.), *Models of madness: Psychological, social, and biological approaches to schizophrenia* (pp. 223-252). New York: Brunner-Routledge.

Read, J., & Ross, C. (2003). Psychological trauma and psychosis: Another reason why people diagnosed schizophrenic must be offered psychological therapies. *Journal of the American Academy of Psychoanalysis and Dynamic Psychiatry, 31,* 247-268.

doi:10.1300/J513v06n02_08

Index